# To Ireland, I

*The Clarendon Lectures in English Literature 1998*

# 'To Ireland, I,

## PAUL MULDOON

WITHDRAW

**OXFORD**
UNIVERSITY PRESS

# OXFORD

UNIVERSITY PRESS

Great Clarendon Street, Oxford OX2 6DP

Oxford University Press is a department of the University of Oxford.
It furthers the University's objective of excellence in research, scholarship,
and education by publishing worldwide in

Oxford New York

Athens Auckland Bangkok Bogotá Buenos Aires Calcutta
Cape Town Chennai Dar es Salaam Delhi Florence Hong Kong Istanbul
Karachi Kuala Lumpur Madrid Melbourne Mexico City Mumbai
Nairobi Paris São Paulo Singapore Taipei Tokyo Toronto Warsaw

with associated companies in Berlin Ibadan

Oxford is a registered trade mark of Oxford University Press
in the UK and in certain other countries

Published in the United States
by Oxford University Press Inc., New York

British Library Cataloguing in Publication Data

Data available

Library of Congress Cataloging in Publication Data

Data available

ISBN 0-19-818475-1

1 3 5 7 9 10 8 6 4 2

Typeset in Dante by
Cambrian Typesetters, Frimley, Surrey

Printed in Great Britain
on acid-free paper by
T. J. International Ltd,
Padstow, Cornwall

*for A. Walton Litz*

# Contents

# I

## 'Wonder-birth'

# Amergin

I begin at the beginning—'like an old ballocks, can you imagine that?'—with the first poems by the first poet of Ireland. According to *Lebor Gabála Érenn*, the twelfth-century 'Book of Invasions', the name of this poet is Amergin. The very first poem attributed to him is composed even as he leaps off a ship, one of the fleet carrying the last great wave of pseudo-historical invaders of Ireland known as the Milesians. I imagine what this boat must look like to the locals, the shadowy Tuatha Dé Danann, particularly now that Amergin wastes no time in letting them know who's in command. For in this first poem Amergin twice uses the term 'I speak for Erin' as he chants of 'Springs of men assembling, | Assembling men at Tara, | Tara, hill of tribes, | Tribes of the son of Míl.'[1] (In this translation, John Montague has very skilfully captured in English the complex link-rhyming of the original.) The term 'Milesians' derives from the name of their leader, the *Míl Espáin*, or 'Spanish Soldier'. His wife, Scota, is an Egyptian pharaoh's daughter, whose name will come to mean 'Irishwoman'. She is the mother of Amergin. This second poem ascribed to him is known as 'The Alphabet Calendar of Amergin':

I am a stag: *of seven tines*
I am a flood: *across a plain*
I am a wind: *on a deep lake*
I am a tear: *the Sun lets fall*
I am a hawk: *above the cliff*
I am a thorn: *beneath the nail*
I am a wonder: *among flowers*
I am a wizard: *who but I*
*Sets the cool aflame with smoke?*

I am a spear: *that rears for blood*
I am a salmon: *in a pool*
I am a lure: *from Paradise*
I am a hill: *where poets walk*
I am a boar: *ruthless and red*

> I am a breaker: *threatening doom*
> I am a tide: *that drags to death*
> I am an infant: *who but I*
> *Peeps from the unhewn dolmen arch?*
>
> I am the womb: *of every holt*
> I am the blaze: *on every hill*
> I am the queen: *of every hive*
> I am the shield: *for every head*
> I am the grave: *of every hope*

The 'grave' in the last line of that translation gives a clue to its provenance. This version of the poem is offered by Robert Graves, who intercuts elements of the poem as it appears in *Lebor Gabála* with a similar poem attributed to the Welsh bard Gwion, better known as Taliesen. In chapter 12 of *The White Goddess*,[2] Graves gives an extraordinary analysis of the significance of this alphabet calendar, connecting initial letters of names of the names to months and the trees associated with those months, so that the 'stag of seven tines', for example, corresponds to the letter B, the month of *Beith*, or the birch, which runs from late December to mid-January. The 'hawk' is related to the letter S, the month of April/May, its tree being the *saille*, or 'willow' of the *salley* gardens in Yeats's poem. The letter associated with the month of June/July and the 'head aflame with smoke' is D, as in *Duir*, the oak tree. 'It is most unlikely,' Graves writes, 'that this poem was allowed to reveal its esoteric meaning to all and sundry; it would have been "pied", as Gwion "pied" his poems, for reasons of security.'[3]

I'd like to suggest that the figure of Amergin is crucial to any understanding of the role of the Irish writer as it has evolved over the centuries. In the first place, he or she seems to have a quite disproportionate sense of his or her own importance, a notion to which I'm doubtless offering no contradictory evidence. The bard Amergin has a mandate, it seems, from the *Míl Espáin* to speak on national issues, to 'speak for Erin'. The tone of the alphabet calendar of Amergin is extraordinarily forthright, in your face. There's no shying away from the large rhetorical gesture, the great public poem. This is, after all, an expeditionary force in whose company he travels, a force that will shortly defeat those previous overlords of Ireland, the Tuatha Dé Danann, at the battles of Tailtiu and Druim Ligen. I'll be focusing on this aspect of the 'public' writer in my second chapter, 'Such a Local Row'. Another aspect of Amergin's poem is, of course, a seemingly contradictory one. It has to do with an urge, equally strong as the public urge, towards what Graves called the 'esoteric' or 'pied'. I assume he's using the word 'pied' in the sense given by the *OED* of a 'mass of type mingled indiscriminately or in confusion, such as results from the breaking down of a forme of type'. That's to say, the urge towards the cryptic, the encoded, the runic, the virtually unintelligible. This will be the subject of my third chapter, 'Alone Tra La', and I'll be relating that cryptic urge to the idea of Amergin's promiscuous provenance and his tireless reinvention of himself as stag or flood or wind or tear or hawk. I should say, of course, that I'm likely to be a little promiscuous myself, referring, when appropriate, to matters other than the one supposedly in hand, though with a tendency to keep coming back to James Joyce's 'The Dead'. And this will be as true of this first chapter as the last, 'Contaygious to the Nile', which will be devoted to the subject of veerings from, over, and back along a line, the notions of di-, trans-, and regression. These four chapters of *To Ireland, I* were delivered, almost exactly as they stand, if in somewhat curtailed forms, over an eight-day period in October and November 1998.

I take my title, 'Wonder-birth', from what is supposedly a direct translation of Amergin's name (the 'gin' is cognate with *genus*), and I take as my theme not only Amergin's magical powers of transformation but his essential liminality, as he stands with an army poised on the threshold of victory. Indeed, he quite forthrightly associates himself with the threshold of an 'unhewn dolmen arch', on which the letters of his alphabet calendar are incised in ogham script. I'd like to focus here on a range of strategies devised by a range of Irish writers for dealing with the ideas of liminality and narthecality that are central, I think, to the Irish experience. As it happens, these writers seem to be lining up just beyond the door, making a kind of alphabet calendar of their own, with all the rigorous randomness, all the random rigour, attending such a plan.

# AE

The first through that oaken *Duir* is someone who would certainly have recognized the root of the word. The great George Russell (1867–1935), otherwise known as AE, writes in his poem 'Exiles':

> The gods have taken alien shapes upon them,
> Wild peasants driving swine
> In a strange country. Through the swarthy faces
> The starry faces shine.

> Under grey tattered skies they strain and reel there:
> Yet cannot disguise
> The majesty of fallen gods, the beauty,
> The fire beneath their eyes.

> They huddle at night within low clay-built cabins;
> And, to themselves unknown,
> They carry with them diadem and sceptre
> And move from throne to throne.[4]

This seems to me to embody a central tenet of the Irish imagination, that what you see is *never* what you get. Heaven and earth are separated by a cloth, albeit a 'tattered' one. There's discrepancy between outward appearance and inward reality. It's what I'm tempted to call 'Eriny'. This notion is nowhere more clearly set down than in AE's 1896 letter to W. B. Yeats:

I am not going to bother you about any derned thing this time but simply to tell you some things about the Ireland behind the veil . . . The gods have returned to Erin and have centred themselves in the sacred mountains and blow the fires through the country. They have been seen by several in vision, they will awaken the magical instinct everywhere, and the universal heart of the people will turn to the old druidic beliefs. I note through the country the increased faith in faery things. The bells are heard from mounds and sounding in the hollows of the mountains.[5]

# Allingham

Let me flesh out this idea of a discrepancy between appearance and reality with a stanza or two from the best-known poem by William Allingham (1824–89):

Up the airy mountain,
  Down the rushy glen,
We daren't go a-hunting,
  For fear of little men;
Wee folk, good folk,
  Trooping all together;
Green jacket, red cap,
  And white owl's feather.

They stole little Bridget
  For seven years long;
When she came back again
  Her friends were all gone.
They took her lightly back,
  Between the night and morrow;
They thought that she was fast asleep,
  But she was dead with sorrow.
They have kept her ever since
  Deep within the lakes,
On a bed of flag-leaves,
  Watching till she wakes.

This idea of there being a contiguous world, a world coterminal with our own, into and out of which some may move, as in Allingham's 'The Fairies', might be traced back to the overthrow of the Tuatha Dé Danann by the Milesians, for after the battles of Tailtiu and Druim Ligen, the Tuatha Dé Danann are literally driven underground. They become the *áes sídhe*, the 'fairy' or 'gentle' folk. They are made invisible by virtue of the *féth fíáda* or *ceo sídhe*, the magic mist or veil, a kind of world-scrim, that hangs about them, often allowing them to appear as animals, particularly deer. In the Fenian cycle of tales, the confrontation with, and crossing over into, a fairy realm often takes place during a hunt with hounds, sometimes to the ringing of bells, as mentioned by AE, or the strains of an unearthly music, or *ceol sídhe*, and it usually involves some kind of time warp. This idea of a parallel universe, a grounded groundlessness, also offers an escape clause, a kind of psychological trapdoor, to a people from under whose feet the rug is constantly being pulled, often quite literally so. Here's Allingham in a more evidently grimmer mode, with a scene of an eviction from his quite brilliant docudrama 'Laurence Bloomfield in Ireland, A Modern Poem':

> In early morning twilight, raw and chill,
> Damp vapours brooding on the barren hill,
> Through miles of mire in steady grave array
> Threescore well-arm'd police pursue their way;
> Each tall and bearded man a rifle swings,
> And under each greatcoat a bayonet clings;
> The Sheriff on his sturdy cob astride
> Talks with the chief, who marches by their side,
> And, creeping on behind them, Paudeen Dhu
> Pretends his needful duty much to rue.
> Six big-boned labourers, clad in common frieze,
> Walk in the midst, the Sherrif's staunch allies;
> Six crowbar men, from distant county brought—
> Orange, and glorying in their work, 'tis thought,
> But wrongly,—churls of Catholics are they,
> And merely hired at half-a-crown a day.

The economy and exactitude of this writing is spectacular. Again, there's a telling image of the 'Six big-boned labourers, clad in common frieze' who embody the idea of the discrepancy between outward and inward. A few lines, later, Allingham moves from the wide-shot to a big close-up:

> One old man, tears upon his wrinkled cheek,
> Stands trembling on a threshold, tries to speak,
> But, in defect of any word for this,
> Mutely upon the doorpost prints a kiss,
> Then passes out for ever.

This image of a critically positioned figure, a figure who is neither here nor there, at some notional interface, may be traced back beyond the immediate context of early to mid-nineteenth-century Ireland ('Laurence Bloomfield in Ireland' was published in 1864) to some deep-seated sense of liminality that was, and is, central to the Irish psyche. The overthrow of the historical counterparts of the pseudo-historical Tuatha Dé Danann by the historical counterparts of the pseudo-historical Milesians, who moved into the country around 500 BC, has been repeated by successive invasions of the country, leaving a sense for many so-called native Irish people of their own invisibility.

## Anonymous

I look to four invisible poets, all of them writing in Irish, on whom I will not linger long just now, though I will return to them anon. The first is the author of *Pairlement Chloinne Tomáis* (The Parliament of Clan Thomas), written sometime in the seventeenth century.[6] This is a political satire, written partly in verse, partly in prose, and presents the genealogy of the loathsome Clan Thomas from their ill-starred origins in hell to ill-starred Munster, where they now hold sway after the demise of what we might call the 'genuine gentry' after the Battle of Kinsale. This anonymous author is familiar with *Lebor Gabála*, so familiar indeed, that he or she includes a parody of its genealogical gyrations. It also parodies the widespread interest in *dinnsheanchas*, or 'the lore of places'. I quote briefly from a translation by Nicholas Williams of a section in which 'droop-eared Murcha O Multuaisgirt', a slovenly scion of the Clan Thomas, prepares to move up in the world by marrying above his station:

'My beloved kinsmen', he said, 'and you intelligent, meticulous and prosperous progeny of Tomas Mor, son of Liobar Lobhtha, son of Lobus Lagrach, son of Dracapeist, son of Beelzebub, I have sent for you for this reason: so that you can advise me what worthy woman I should take to wife; for it is high time that I marry a woman after and since the death of my wife, the love of my heart, namely: Brighid Ni Magarlain, daughter of Mathghamhain Breallach O Magarlain and tawny-legged Raghnuit Ni Mheigiollain from Ballydehob.' [Generation and *re*generation is much in the air here, since the word *magairle* means 'scrotum' or 'testicles'.] And when he had spoken these words, a mucous stream of tears fell from him and a seizure and sorrow of heart took hold of him, so that he could not speak for a while. 'Now I hear,' said Murcha, 'that there is a prosperous chieftain in fair and lovely Connaught, namely: Maghnus O Madagain . . . and this same Maghnus has a beautiful virgin daughter, and I have decided with your approval to send messengers to ask her father for her hand.'

The name of the 'beautiful virgin daughter' turns out to be Meadhbh, a direct reference to the queen of Connaught who, with her husband,

*Aillil*, is a key figure in the great Irish epic *Táin Bó Cuailgne*. Despite advice to the contrary from his druids (the priests of the *Duir*), Maghnus O Madagain allows his daughter to marry 'droop-eared Murcha O Multuaisgirt':

and the girl was joined to him in marriage, namely, Meadhbh, daughter of Maghnus by name; and he took her off with him to his own house and many children were engendered by them that night.

I'll leave the highly 'Erinized' end of this episode from *Pairlement Chloinne Tomáis* for the moment, and turn to my second anonymous poet, a woman, almost certainly the wife of the king mentioned in the poem. This king is Áed Mac Ainmirech, a historical figure killed in 598 AD. Tailtiu, scene of that great battle between the Tuatha Dé Danann and the Milesians, would become the site of a royal palace, like the hill of Tara. The translation here is by Thomas Kinsella:

> Three rounded flanks I loved
> and never will see again:
> the flank of Tara, the flank of Tailtiu
> and the flank of Áed Mac Ainmirech.[7]

It's as if there's no distinction between public and private, between event large and event small. This, I'm certain, is partly a function of the size of Ireland, a country in which a blaze on the hill of Tara or Tailtiu (modern Teltown), the kind of blaze Amergin might embody, would be visible over great distances. It's on his way to light a fire, metaphorically if not literally, at the great meeting point of Tara, of course, that St Patrick himself avails of the *féth fiada* and turns himself and his acolyte, Benen, into deer so as to escape an ambush.

My third anonymous poet is probably writing in the ninth century:

> *Int én bec*
> *ro léic feit*
> *do rind guip*
>     *glanbuid*
>
> *fo-cird faíd*
> *ós Loch Laíg*
> *lon do chraíb*
>     *charnbuidi*

This translation of 'The Blackbird over Belfast Lough' is by Gerard Murphy: 'The little bird which has whistled from the end of a bright-yellow bill: it utters a note above Belfast Loch—a blackbird from a yellow-heaped branch.'[8]

My fourth anonymous poet is also writing out of the ninth century. These are three verses from his poem in praise of 'May-Day':

> *Cerbaid sam*
> *súaill sruth,*
> *saigid graig*
> > *lúath linn;*
> *lethaid folt*
> *fota fraích,*
> *for-beir canach*
> > *fann finn.*
>
> *Berait beich*
> *(becc a nert)*
> *bert bond,*
> > *bochtai bláith;*
> *beirid buar*
> *slaibre slíab,*
> *feraid seng*
> > *saidbir sáith.*
>
> *Greit mer fort*
> *imrimm ech*
> *imma-sernar*
> > *sreth slúag;*
> *ro-saerad crann*
> *gel is-tir,*
> *co ni di ór*
> > *eilestair úad.*

As is evident from the translation, again by Gerard Murphy, this anonymous poet has a terrific trust in the things of this world. He's content to focus on what's immediately to hand, rather than strive for something beyond:

Summer cuts the stream small; swift horses seek water; tall heather spreads; delicate fair foliage flourishes . . . Bees of small strength carry bundles of culled blossom on their feet; the mountain, supplying rich sufficiency, carries off the cattle . . . Woodland music plays; melody provides perfect peace; dust is blown from dwelling-place, and haze from lake full of water . . . Fierce ardour and riding of horses; the serried host is ranged around; the pond is noble in bounty and turns the iris to gold.[9]

## Beckett

I want to cross-fade from that image of the 'iris', or 'flag', to another flaggy shore:

We drifted in among the flags and stuck. The way they went down, sighing, before the stem! (*Pause.*) I lay down across her with my face in her breasts and my hand on her. We lay there without moving. But under us all moved, and moved us, gently, up and down, and from side to side.[10]

The man 'trembling on the threshold' here is of course Krapp, the creation of the Lord of Liminality himself. Samuel Beckett (1906–89) was so much taken by resonances of his own name that he would surely have delighted in that phrase in the anonymous ninth-century poem, written in the language of which Molloy speaks, 'tears and laughter, they are so much Gaelic to me':[11]

> *Berait beich*
> *(becc a nert)*

While the word *beich* means 'bees' in this context, it is cognate with a number of sharp-ended or pointed things, including *boc*, a 'he-goat' and *bac*, a word Dinneen in his great dictionary, published in 1927, gives as meaning, in Modern Irish, 'a quirk; an angular space, hollow or object; a river turn; a crozier, a mattock, a billhook, a prop, a pin, a crook, a peg, a thole-pin; a joint, a hook; a shackle, a hindrance, a stop; a fire-hop, a fire-prop, corner of hob; act of supporting, holding back, hindering'.[12] The word *becc* means 'little, small, tiny or few'. In other words, *Beich becc* is a version of the 'diminutive beaked thing' of Beckett's own name. I'd like to suggest that Beckett was familiar not only with this poem but with that other ninth-century poem about 'The Blackbird Over Belfast Lough', both of which appear, with their original texts, in Gerard Murphy's *Early Irish Lyrics* (1956). The first line of 'The Blackbird', if you recall, reads '*Int en bec*'. Here *bec* refers quite specifically to the 'beak' or 'bill' of the blackbird. I'm reminded, though, of that passage in *Malone Dies* in which Mr and Mrs Saposcat ponder the presentation of a pen to their schoolboy son, Sapo:

One day Mr Saposcat sold himself a fountain-pen, at a discount. A Bird. I shall give it to him on the morning of the examination, he said. He took off the long cardboard lid and showed the pen to his wife. Leave it in its box! he cried, as she made to take it in her hand. It lay almost hidden in the scrolled leaflet containing the instructions for use. Mr Saposcat parted the edges of the paper and held up the box for his wife to look inside. But she, instead of looking at the pen, looked at him. He named the price. Might it not be better, she said, to let him have it the day before, to give him time to get used to the nib? You are right, he said, I had not thought of that. Or even two days before, she said, to give him time to change the nib if it does not suit him.

I'll not linger over the sexual under- or overtones in this passage, spoken by a character who has just written of his pencil: 'I must have had it about me when I was brought here. It has five faces. It is very short. It is pointed at both ends. A Venus. I hope it will see me out.'[13] But there is certainly an absolute identification between the pen, a word cognate with the word *binn*, a 'peak' (the name of St Patrick's acolyte, Benen, probably allows for his transmogrification into a 'peaked' deer) and *le bec*, the nib with which Beckett himself wrote in French, and the character of Saposcat. That 'Ill-starred punster',[14] as Joyce calls 'Sam' in *Finnegans Wake*, now focuses on the pen and its *bec* with extraordinary attention:

A bird, its yellow beak agape to show it was singing, adorned the lid, which Mr Saposcat now put on again. He wrapped with expert hands the box in tissue paper and slipped over it a narrow rubber band. He was not pleased. It is a medium nib, he said, and it will certainly suit him.[15]

This 'bird, its yellow beak agape to show it was singing' is surely that same bird that perched on the mountainside over Belfast Lough, the mountain with which Beckett would have been all-too-familiar from his sojourn as a teacher at Campbell College. (It sounds as if young Sapo might be one of those Campbell College schoolboys Beckett

described as '*la crème de la crème* . . . rich and thick'.) The essence of
Sapo's gift-to-be, should he successfully undergo his rite of passage
and pass his exam, is obscured by a series of barriers or scrims. The
first of these is the 'lid' of the box, of course. Then there's the 'tissue
paper', followed by the prophylactic 'rubber band'. This wrapping
and unwrapping of a 'box', in conjunction with the word 'band', connects the scene in *Malone Dies* with the scene in *La Dernière Bande*, the
French title of *Krapp's Last Tape* that may famously be rendered in
English not only as 'The Last Tape' but 'The Last Erection'. As Krapp
reflects on his own reflections (the brilliant theatrical device of the
tape recorder leaves him at one remove from the details of his past life,
yet absolutely engaged with them) he thinks of the prowess of
another 'beak'. This is the 'stem' of Krapp's punt, yet another version
of a *beak* as defined by the *OED* as 'the pointed and ornamental pro-
jection at the prow of ancient vessels':

We drifted in among the flags and stuck. The way they went down, sighing,
before the stem!

I'm tempted to suggest that, at this Proustian moment (*la proue, la
prouesse*), with its embodiment of moving and not moving, being and
not being, Beckett is hearking back to Allingham's image-field in 'The
Fairies', with his description of little Bridget:

> They took her lightly back,
>     Between the night and morrow;
> They thought that she was fast asleep,
>     But she was dead with sorrow.
> They have kept her ever since
>     Deep within the lakes,
> On a bed of flag-leaves,
>     Watching till she wakes.

This last image of the watcher is echoed by Krapp:

I said again I thought it was hopeless and no good going on, and she agreed,
without opening her eyes. (*Pause.*) I asked her to look at me and after a few
moments—(*pause*)—after a few moments she did, but the eyes just slits,
because of the glare. I bent over her to get them in the shadow and they
opened. (*Pause. Low.*) Let me in. We drifted in among the flags and stuck. The
way they went down, sighing, before the stem! (*Pause.*) I lay down across her

with my face in her breasts and my hand on her. We lay there without moving. But under us all moved, and moved us, gently, up and down, and from side to side.[16]

I'm struck, as I revisit that passage, by the positioning of the word 'gently'. It seems to me to be the key to the ghostly presence of Allingham's *gentle* folk and the chilling vigil they keep for little Bridget. The 'flags' are significant in several further senses. The word 'flag' is commonly used of rushes, so connecting it to rush crosses of the cult of St Brigid, the 'rushy glen' of the first stanza of Allingham's poem, and the rushes in Job 8: 7–11:

> Question the meditation that has passed,
>> meditate on the experience of its ancestors—
> for we children of yesterday, we know nothing,
>> our life on earth passes like a shadow—
> but they will teach you, they will tell you,
>> and their thought is expressed in these sayings,
> 'Can papyrus flourish except in marshes?
> Without water can the rushes grow?'

I set 'our life on earth passes like a shadow' side by side with's Krapp's 'I bent over to get them in the shadow'. As we know, Beckett is here alluding to the device of the *gnomon* used by Joyce in the stories of *Dubliners*, so that the figure of Krapp becomes a sundial stick casting a shadow. 'Bethicket him for a stump of a beech', the master had written of Beckett in *Finnegans Wake*,[17] picking up on an irreverent line of Swift on Wood, but pointing to another aspect of Beckett's name, its own essential 'woodiness'. For the *bec* may be construed as a version of the Old English *boc*, a 'beech', a word that lies behind 'book'. Beckett is thereby both pen and paper. Krapp identifies himself with the 'stem' of the punt, and 'stem' and 'stump' are etymologically linked. Moreover, the Beckett who strove so vehemently to have his birthdate coincide with a Good Friday must have experienced a certain frisson when he read in 'The Fairies':

> By the craggy hill-side,
>> Through the mosses bare,
> They have planted thorn-trees
>> For pleasure here and there.

> If any man so daring
>   As dig one up in spite,
> He shall find their sharpest thorns
>   In his bed at night.

We might remember Pozzo's sense of a 'wonder-birth', his assertion in *Waiting for Godot* that 'They give birth astride a grave, the light gleams an instant, then it's night once more', an idea picked up by Vladimir, 'Astride of a grave and a difficult birth. Down in the hole, lingeringly, the grave digger puts on the forceps'.[18] We might linger ourselves a moment over those 'forceps', since they correspond to yet another *OED* definition of *beak*, 'a pair of pincers, a forceps', before moving on to consider the 'gleam' of the flag-iris, a flower known in Modern Irish as *feileastram* or, more tellingly, *soileastar*, with its connotations of *solas*, 'light' or 'a window', its faint echo of *clap-sholas*, or twilight, the medium of the clapped-out Krapp. The Irish word crap itself is used exclusively in compounds and means 'shrivelled, crippled, gathered up', a sense that would correspond with Beckett's striking stage-direction description of Krapp as 'wearish'. The strongest contender for the provenance of the name, however, might be a usage in the 'May-Day' poem:

> Gairid cui
> chrúaidh den;
> is fo-chen
>     sam sáir:
> suidid sine
> serb
> i mbi cerb
>     caill chraíb.

The hardy vigorous cuckoo calls. Welcome to noble summer: it abates the bitterness of storm during which branchy wood is lacerated.[19]

I want to suggest that both *cerb* and *chraíb* are both near versions of 'Krapp' and that Beckett is not only conscious of the meaning of *cerb* as 'lacerated' but has read Murphy's gloss on the word, with its suggestion that the word is cognate with the 'Scottish gallic noun *cearb*, "rag, tatter . . . imperfect or ragged piece of dress . . . defect" '. He's conscious, too, of *chraíb*, 'a branch', so that Krapp, like his creator, becomes the 'stem' of the punt. If Beckett was indeed familiar with Murphy's *Early Irish Lyrics*, using them as an image store for some idyllic world, he must also have delighted here in a stanza in which his own name, *sam*, appears as 'summer'. But I disgress. The final sense of the flag or iris, with which this passage is 'pied', is runic in a way Amergin would have recognized. I should mention, by the way, that there are two Amergins or Amairgins in Irish literature. We've already met the son of Mil. The second Amairgin is also a poet, the son of Conall Carnach and the brother-in-law of Connor MacNessa, the Ulster king who supposedly died on Good Friday. Among Amairgin's exploits are the killing of a monster at Cruachan, the hill palace of Medhbh and Ailill, the aforementioned queen and king of Connaught. I'm pretty sure that Beckett is thinking of this Cruachan when he has Krapp ponder how he might 'be again on Croghan on a Sunday morning, in the haze, with the bitch, stop and listen to the bells'. This is the conventional prelude to an occasion of *féth fíada*. There's the 'haze' or *ceo sídhe*, the 'bells' or *ceol sidhe*, and the 'bitch', the hunting dog which raises and tracks the phantom deer, as the memory of the girl on the punt is about to be raised and tracked. That 'haze' also goes back to the '*haze* from lake full of water' in the Murphy translation of 'May-Day', the title of which would already have a cryptic significance for Beckett since the name of his mother was, of course, May. We know that there's a strong connection between the historical events surrounding May Beckett's death and the image in *Krapp's Last Tape* of 'the blind went down, one of those dirty brown roller affairs'.[20] This 'blind' is itself a version of the world-scrim. But I disgress again. I was thinking of the word 'iris', how it's a near version of 'Irish'. And I'm suggesting that this is the encrypted word that allows a reader to open the portal on this passage in Beckett, particularly with its Gaelic underpinning. While 'tears and laughter' may be 'so much Gaelic' to Molloy, they are meat and drink to his creator. 'But here I am back at my old aporetics',[21] as Malone writes of himself, 'Is that the word? I don't know.' Krapp combines Lucky's 'divine aphasia',[22] the condition of being 'unable to speak' with what one might term Malone's 'divine aporia', the condition of being 'full of doubts'. The speaker of *The Unnamable*, meanwhile, wonders 'Are there other places set aside for us and this one where I am, with Malone, merely their narthex?'[23] A 'narthex', I remind myself, is 'properly the name of a tall, umbiliferous plant with a hollow stalk'—a 'stem', you might say—'also, a small case or casket for unguents'. The primary definition, though, is 'a vestibule or portico stretching across the western end of some early Christian churches and basilicas, divided from the nave by a wall, screen or railing, and set apart for the use of women, catechumens, penitents and other persons; an ante-nave'. It is in this space that Malone and Krapp would recognize a fellow feeling for Allingham's 'old man, tears upon his wrinkled cheek' who 'stands trembling on a threshold', who 'tries to speak, | But, in defect of any word for this, | Mutely upon the door-post prints a kiss, | Then passes out for ever.'

## Bowen

Beckett's magisterial final addendum in 'Addenda (1)'—there is no (2)—to his "Big House" novel, *Watt*, reads 'no symbols where none intended'.[24] The same holds true of the work of Elizabeth Bowen (1899–1973). I'll concentrate on two short stories, 'The Tommy Crans' and 'The Demon Lover',[25] that give new twists and twitches to the idea of the veiled and the unveiled. 'The Demon Lover' is the story of a certain Mrs Drover, who returns to her shut-up house in wartime London (her family has been packed off to the country):

In her once familiar street, as in any unused channel, an unfamiliar queerness had silted up; a cat wove itself in and out of railings, but no human eye watched Mrs Drover's return. Shifting some parcels under her arm, she slowly forced round her latchkey in an unwilling lock, then gave the door, which had warped, a push with her knee. Dead air came out to meet her as she went in.

The combination of the words 'familiar' and 'cat' summon up a witch's 'familiar', the other-worldly atmosphere compounded by the detail that 'no human eye watched Mrs Drover's return'. The comparison of the cat that 'wove itself in and out of railings' to a shuttle in a loom brings with it not only the idea of immanence from Job 7: 6

('My days are swifter than a weaver's shuttle, and are spent without hope') but once again sets up the idea of a scrim between one world and another. The 'railings' delineate a narthex, though the door opens less into a nave than a crypt, pointing to further encryption. The ominous nature of things extends even to a version of *nomen est omen* implicit in Mrs Drover's name. The 'D' of 'Demon' and the 'over' of 'Lover' are built into 'Drover'. It is fated that Mrs Drover meet her demon lover at the hair-raising end of the story. Mrs Drover passes through a number of world-scrims, rooms in which 'though not much dust had seeped in, each object wore a film of another kind', pondering all the while if the caretaker has returned to leave the letter on the hall table, thinking back to the evening of her soldier fiancé's leave-taking for the Great War, until she flees the house and boards the only taxi in the taxi rank:

This evening, only one taxi—but this, although it presented its black rump, appeared already to be alertly waiting for her. Indeed, without looking round the driver started his engine as she panted up from behind and put her hand on the door. As she did so, the clock struck seven.

It's remarkable that this moment again corresponds so neatly to the convention of the *féth fiada*. The taxi with its 'black rump' is the equivalent of a deer. Mrs Drover 'panted up from behind' like a hound giving chase. There is a sound effect of the clock, the *ceol sídhe*, delineating the moment.

The driver braked to what was almost a stop, turned round and slid the glass panel back: the jolt of this flung Mrs Drover forward till her face was almost into the glass. Through the aperture driver and passenger, not six inches between them, remained for an eternity eye to eye. Mrs Drover's mouth remained open for some time before she could issue her first scream. After that she continued to scream freely and to beat with her gloved hands on the glass all around as the taxi, accelerating without mercy, made off with her into the hinterland of deserted streets.

The taxi here corresponds to the encapsulating *ceo sídhe*, or otherworldly mist, in which Mrs Drover is spirited away by her 'driver'. The combination of 'Drover' (a word that is used specifically of driving cattle, and is therefore a gloss on the *bo* element in Bowen's name) and the 'driver' with its connotations of what is 'driven'—rain or snow—brings me back to a key sentence, the last, if you recall, in the first paragraph of 'The Demon Lover':

Dead air came out to meet her as she went in.

The positioning of the word 'dead' here points in the direction of what can only be the ghost text of this story, James Joyce's 'The Dead'.[26] The 'snow' that is general over Ireland in Joyce is replaced here by 'rain'. The focus on the 'caretaker' throughout the Bowen reminds us of the central role of 'Lily, the caretaker's daughter' in Joyce. The letter on the hall table is a version of the 'heliotrope envelope' Gabriel Conroy remembers from his 'secret life' with Gretta. The positioning of Mrs Drover with her lover 'in the garden . . . under a tree . . . looking in through the window at her mother and sister' precisely replicates Gretta's memory of that last night she saw Michael Furey, the night 'the window was so wet I couldn't see so I ran downstairs as I was and slipped out the back into the garden and there was the poor fellow at the end of the garden, shivering . . . He was standing at the end of the wall where there was a tree.' The 'driver' in Bowen is prefigured in 'the cabman' in Joyce, who drives Gabriel and Gretta to the Gresham hotel, the neutral ground in which Gabriel realizes that 'one by one they were all becoming shades'.

The second Bowen story, 'The Tommy Crans', begins with the following sentence:

Herbert's feet, from dangling so long in the tram, had died of cold in his boots; he stamped the couple of coffins on blue-and-buff mosaic.

Yet again, this is a remake of the first sentence of 'The Dead':

Lily, the caretaker's daughter, was literally run off her feet.

The point of view of both Lily and Herbert are presented by their colloquialisms—'literally run off her feet' and the 'couple of coffins'. Those 'couple of coffins' allude also to how Gabriel 'stretched himself cautiously along under the sheets and lay down beside his wife' in a way reminiscent of the monks at Mount Mellary who 'slept in their coffins', while the phrase 'died of cold' describes exactly what happened to Michael Furey, as would befit yet another character for whom *nomen est omen*. The name Furey echoes the Irish words *fuar*, meaning 'cold' and *faobhar*, an 'edge', while the term *faobhar an dhorais* means quite specifically a 'threshold', the threshold upon which the Lass of Aughrim sings. 'The Lass of Aughrim' is also known as 'The Lass of Loch Royal' or, given the slippage between 'l' and 'n', 'The Lass of Loch Royan':

> The rain falls on my yellow locks
> And the dew it wets my skin;
> My babe lies cold in my arms;
> Lord Gregory let me in.

This 'let me in' is, I suggest, the 'let me in' of the punting Krapp. While the clues are all there in that compacted first sentence about 'Herbert's feet', the second, third, and fourth sentences will confirm the Joycean connection, most immediately in the setting:

In the Tommy Crans' cloak-room the pegs were too high—uncle Archer cocked H.M.S. *Terrible* for him over a checked ulster. Tommy Cran—aslant, meanwhile, in the doorway, was an enormous presence. 'Come on, now, come!' he exclaimed, and roared with impatience. You would have said he was also arriving at the Tommy Crans' Christmas party, of which one could not bear to miss a moment.

Scarcely is the story under way than we sense that if 'In the Tommy Crans' cloak-room the pegs were too high' then it's more likely than not that the Tommy Crans will be brought down a peg or two—might I say, a *bec* or two?—which is precisely how the story evolves. My mention of the peg/*bec* syndrome leads me to ponder the very name of 'the Tommy Crans': Bowen again loads the name 'Cran' with an extraordinary freight, again using a version of *nomen est omen*. Dinneen gives five main areas of definition of the Irish word *crann*: 1. a tree. (You might remember this meaning from the anonymous seventh-century poem we read earlier—*ro-saered crann | gel is-tir*, 'the white tree has been ennobled in the land'.) 2. a bole, mast, shaft; a bolt, a bar, a beam; a stave, a timber. 3. a wooden vessel, frame, device, etc. 4. a lot, a piece of stick used in casting lots. 5. a tune, a melody, a step in dancing; *cf. Eng.* bar, stave. That first sentence describing Tommy Cran is worth another look, I think, particularly when its rather awkward syntax so draws attention to itself, mimetic as it is of Tommy's skewdness:

Tommy Cran—aslant, meanwhile, in the doorway, was an enormous presence.

Again, it's as if Tommy Cran is fated to become the bole, bolt, bar, or barrier on his own threshold, so that we're not sure if he's welcoming us or warding us off, just as it's not clear if he's coming or going. The 'cloak' in the narthecal 'cloak-room' opens into a magical place:

The room where they all sat seemed to be made of glass, it collected the whole daylight; the candles were still waiting. Over the garden, day still hung like a pink flag; over the trees like frozen feathers, the enchanted icy lake, the lawn. The table was in the window. As Herbert was brought in the clock struck four.

I want to suggest that, yet again, Bowen presents us with a *féth fiada*, again signalled by a clock striking, in which concepts of 'here' and 'there' are problematized—'The table was in the window'. There is a persistent, consistent, hunt imagery running through the piece, signalled by a world-scrim falling:

So the coloured candles were lit, the garden went dark with loneliness and was immediately curtained out. Two of the uncles put rugs on and bounded about the room like bears and lions.

After tea, when Herbert and Nancy go and stand by the lake, glimpsing in the distance the 'uncles *chasing* the laughing aunts', Nancy says, ' "I never believed in fairies—did you either?" ' and, shortly afterwards, gives him a present of 'something really her own, a pink glass greyhound', the archetypical hunting dog. The lake has already been identified with 'two swans', birds emblematic of an other-worldly interface, as in the metamorphosis of the children of Lir, upon whom a spell is cast so that they disappear for three hundred years and return to Ireland as decrepit old people, a lake on which, in a prefiguring of the decrepit Krapp's punt-vision, Herbert thinks of Nancy:

how, in summer, her boat would go pushing among the lily-leaves. She showed him their boat-house, rusty-red from a lamp inside, solid. 'We had a lamp put there for the poor cold swans.' (And the swans were asleep beside it.)

I can't prove it, of course, but I'd be willing to bet that Beckett is conscious of this passage in Bowen, particularly when the sequence of Krapp's taped reverie about Croghan (from *cruach*, a crook or rick, Croghan is a near homonym for *crann*), the haze, the bitch, the bells, the drifting in among the flags, is immediately preceded by 'Be again in the dingle on a Christmas Eve, gathering holly, the *red*-berried.'[27] That reference to the swans is followed immediately by a series of questions about time, mortality, and generation:

'How old are you, Herbert?'
'Eight.'
'Oh, I'm nine. Do you play brigands?'
'I could,' said Herbert.
'Oh, I don't; I'd hate to.'

The combination of 'brigands' (cognate with the *Brigantiae* and their bear-deity,[28] the rush-crossed little St *Brig*id) and the 'rusty-red' in the boathouse conjures up an association with the hunting, shooting, fishing Red Branch Knights, 'Red Branch' here referring to the hall, the *Craobh Rua*, often identified as Creeveroe in County Armagh, in which the knights rested up with their leader, the aforementioned Connor Mac Nessa, where they were no doubt entertained by the aforementioned second Amairgin. I'll come back to the Red Branch Knights when I look at Joyce's 'The Dead' in more detail. For the moment, let me suggest that the focus on time passing, if not indeed the concept of a time warp associated with the *féth fiada*, is consistent with Bowen's interest in, and deft handling of, time in this six-page story, so densely packed that, by the time one reaches the end, one has the sense of having read sixty, perhaps even six hundred, pages:

As they turned back to face the window, her smile and voice were tender, but not for him. In the brightly lit stripped room the Tommy Crans walked about together, like lovers in their freedom from one another. They talked of the fortune to be made, the child to be born. Tommy flung his chest out and moved his arms freely in air he did not possess; here and there, pink leaflets fluttered into the dark. The Tommy Crans would go on for ever and be continued; their seed would never fail.

This revisiting of the end of 'The Dead', with the similar blocking of the scene between Gabriel and Gretta and the substitution of 'pink leaflets' from some get-rich-quick scheme for the snow, 'flakes, silver and dark, falling obliquely against the lamplight' is no less sustained, of course, than the 'Eriny', or discrepancy between appearance and reality. For we know that the 'seed' of the 'Tommy Crans' will *most certainly* fail. The 'Eriny' is every bit as heavy as the description of the wedding night, with its wondrous multiple engenderings, in *Pairlement Chloinne Tomáis*, a text to which, I suggest, Bowen quite blatantly alludes in substituting 'The Tommy Crans' for 'Clan Thomas', a function of that common slippage between 'r' and 'l'. This further 'Erinizes' the fate of 'The Tommy Crans', the dispossessed Anglo-Irish 'gentry' who are turning, again because of that slippage between 'r' and 'l', into possessing 'gentles', ghosts of themselves who are implicated in, but cut off from, their own lives.

I've dwelt at length here on Bowen's revisiting the anonymous author of *Pairlement Chloinne Tomáis* and her slanted acknowledgement of Joyce as a figure who, like 'Tommy Cran—aslant, meanwhile, in the doorway—was an enormous presence'. I've dwelt on the recurring image of that liminal place. I've dwelt on the recurring image of the narthex, what one might call the terminal narthecality not only of so many of Beckett's characters but so many characters in Irish literature. I've dwelt on Beckett's revisiting Bowen and Allingham. I've dwelt on the idea of the recurring image of a *féth fiada*, the barrier between being and not-being, between this world and some other, wondrous realm, often manifesting itself as a mist, of course, but just as often taking the form of a woven fabric, a 'textile'. I've dwelt on the complexity, sometimes the complicatedness, of so many of these 'texts' and their 'subtexts'. Now I'd like to suggest that the extraordinary appetite and aptitude for 'intertextuality' among these writers goes beyond a mere interest in the allusive, or the parodic, but is symptomatic of several deep-seated senses. The first is of concomitancy. There's a sense of two discrete coexistent realms. Two texts. Concomitant with that, though, is the fact there's no distinction between one world and the next. Or one text and the next. If there's a fine line between the notions of 'allusiveness' and 'elusiveness', it's so fine it's constantly breaking down. Concomitant with that is a touching disregard for the figure of the author. Joyce belongs in Bowen,

Bowen, Allingham, and those anonymous ninth-century Irish poets in Beckett. All, indeed, are anonymous. Their very disregard for their 'selves' allows them to mutate and transmogrify themselves, to position themselves, with Amergin, at some notional cutting edge.

## Carleton

I'll look briefly at three or four writers who are, to a greater or lesser extent, part of an avant-garde, a term with militaristic connotations recognizable to Amergin but otherwise now all but forgotten. These writers are shock-troopers of sorts, however unlikely that may seem as a description of William Carleton (1794–1857). Shock-trooper or, more accurately, double agent, a mover behind enemy lines, a man with a foot in both camps, Carleton represents an extraordinary straddling of the two main religio-political traditions in Ireland. Born and brought up as an Irish-speaking Roman Catholic in County Tyrone, a member of the secret society of the Ribbonmen, Carleton would convert—should I say 'defect'?—to Protestantism shortly after his move to Dublin in the 1820s. By the time he'd published his first story, 'The Lough Dearg Pilgrim', in 1828, Carleton's new-found anti-Catholic sentiment was firmly in place:

There is no specimen of Irish superstition equal to that which is to be seen at St. Patrick's Purgatory, in Lough Dearg. A devout Romanist who has not made a pilgrimage to this place can scarcely urge a bold claim to the character of piety . . . It is melancholy to perceive the fatal success to which the Church of Rome has attained, in making void the atonement of Christ by her traditions; and how every part of her complicated, but perfect, system, even to the minutest points, seizes upon some corresponding weakness of the human heart, thereby to bind it to her agreeable and strong delusions.[29]

Carleton contains a powerful combination of intimacy with, and enmity towards, his subject matter that would not be seen again until Joyce, where it's the one stunningly simple quality that makes 'The Dead' so stunningly complex. We know that Joyce was interested in revisiting Carleton from his letter to Stanislaus Joyce of 6 November 1906:

I have written to A[unt] J[osephine] asking her . . . to try to lay hands on any old editions of Kickham, Griffin, *Carleton*, H. J. Smyth &c, Banim and to send me a Xmas present made up of tram-tickets, advts, handbills, posters, papers, programmes &c. I would like to have a map of Dublin on my wall. I suppose I am becoming a maniac. I am writing her today to know how you spell Miss McCleod's (?) Reel.[30]

As Richard Ellmann points out in his note, the detail of Miss McCleod's Reel, 'probably intended for "The Dead", was not used'.[31] Though Ellman doesn't say why, I would suggest that it's because Joyce doesn't want his reader to summon up the McCleod of the moment—that's to say the recently deceased 'Fiona Macleod', the pseudonym and alter ego of William Sharp (1855–1905), champion of the 'new paganism', with its insistence that 'a new epoch is about to be inaugurated' now that 'the religion of our forefathers' has waned. It simply isn't 'a gentle way of putting it',[32] as Joyce describes his method in the following sentence, citing the example of how 'I have also added in the story *The Clay* the name of Maria's laundry, the *Dublin by Lamplight Laundry*.' A few paragraphs later, we hear a familiar Carletonian note being struck, including his unconscious repetition of the word 'peasantry' from Carleton's *Traits and Stories of the Irish Peasantry*:

The Irish proletariat has yet to be created. A feudal peasantry exists, scraping the soil but this would with a national revival or with a definite preponderance of England surely disappear. I quite agree with you that Griffith is afraid of the priests—and he has every reason to be so. But, possibly, they are also a little afraid of him too. After all, he is holding out some secular liberty to the people and the Church doesn't approve of that. I quite see, of course, that the church is still, as it was in the time of Adrian IV, the enemy of Ireland: but, I think, her time is almost up.[33]

I suspect that, had Aunt Josephine met Joyce's request, the story she's most likely to have sent him is 'The Midnight Mass', in which Owen Reillaghan labours through a snowstorm in search of the supposed murderer of his brother, Mike:

At first he struggled heroically with the storm; but when utter darkness threw its impervious *shades* over the desolation around him, and the *fury* of the elements grew so tremendous, all the strong propensities to life became roused . . . These struggles, however, as well as those of the body, became gradually weaker as the storm tossed him about, and with the *chill* of his breath *withered* him into total helplessness . . . The tumult of the tempest, the whirling of the snow-clouds, and the *thick snow, now falling* and again tossed upwards by sudden gusts to the clouds, deprived him of all power of reflection . . . The driving sleet and hard granular snow now ceased to fall; but were succeeded by large feathery flakes, that *descended* slowly upon the still air.[34]

I suggest that this particular storm is at least as strong a contender for the provenance of the snow-scene at the end of 'The Dead' as the much-vaunted opening of Bret Harte's *Gabriel Conroy*, though the latter's obviously the provenance of Gabriel's name. My reason for this has to do with several aspects of the Carleton. The first is the combination of the shared vocabulary, italicized above. Then there's the intellectual and emotional crisis in the protagonist of which the storm is the outward manifestation. Thirdly, there's the iconography of 'the Mass performed under the open sky' on Christmas Eve, which is picked up by Joyce on the Feast of the Epiphany, in the 'crooked crosses', the 'spears' and the 'thorns' at the midnight culmination of his story. I'm fairly sure, too, that Joyce was familiar with 'The Midnight Mass' because of the key moment in the plot-line, in which it transpires that Mike shares some of the same qualities as the great Tim Finnegan, so that 'a deep groan was heard, and the apparently dead man opened his eyes, and feebly exclaimed—"a dhrink! A dhrink!" '.[35]

## Coffey

Those same qualities for radical self-renewal found in Mike Reillaghan and his creator are also to be found in Brian Coffey (1905–95), a poet intent on walking the fine, liminal-narthecal line between continuity and discontinuity, location and dislocation. Like many mould-breakers, Coffey is thought of, if he's thought of at all, as a 'difficult' poet. As his editor, J. C. C. Mays, points out in his introduction to Coffey's *Poems and Versions 1929–1990*:

If Coffey's poems get difficult, it is because his stance is difficult to maintain—difficult for him and his readers—but it is difficult because there are no props, not because there are props which require further props of explanation . . . It should therefore come as no surprise that Coffey's writing provokes resistance, even resentment. It will puzzle or cause affront to anyone who thinks poetry exists on the side, as an adjunct or comfortable adornment.[36]

# Devlin

The same might be said of Denis Devlin (1908–59), with whom Coffey shared his first book of poems, entitled *Poems*, self-published by the pair of them in 1930. Like many mould-breakers, Devlin is thought of, if he's thought of at all, as a 'difficult' poet. As his editor, J. C. C. Mays, points out in his introduction to the *Collected Poems of Denis Devlin*:

When the method is not understood it looks like the product of disabling detachment, snobbery. Devlin's way of handling ordinary syntactic transitions might appear to be the product of impatience, but the estimate equally would be wrong. Sense is elided, meaning is syncopated, because it has to be.[37]

While Coffey and Devlin were described by Beckett in his 1934 *Bookman* review as 'without question the most interesting of the youngest generation of Irish poets', it's difficult not to see them as sticks which Beckett might use to beat the 'leading twilighters',[38] particularly Yeats, who dwell in the *clap-sholas*, while giving themselves over to the influences of 'the *surrealistes* and Mr Eliot, perhaps also those of Mr Pound'. Beckett might well have mentioned the name of Mr Joyce, to whom Devlin alludes in his best-known poem, 'Lough Derg':

> Against the craftsmen's primary-coloured skies
> Whose gold was *Gabriel* on the patient roofs,
> The parabled windows taught *the dead* to rise.[39]

I suspect that Beckett himself is thinking of 'Lough Derg' in some of the details of *Krapp's Last Tape*, particularly the punt scene on the lake, a site which, like Lough Derg, allows for the possibility of spiritual recovery. St Patrick is already a ghost in the scene, through the place name 'Croghan', which brings to mind the other great Irish pilgrimage to *Croagh* Patrick, while the play is written specifically with *Patrick* Magee's voice in mind. That Lough Derg, 'the red lake', might be in Beckett's mind, at least subliminally, is suggested by 'holly, the red-berried'.[40] Several word choices of Beckett also found in 'Lough Derg' include the 'berries' and, just a few lines before, 'Behind the eyes the winged ascension flags'.[41] This line includes two central ideas in *Krapp's Last Tape*. The first is the idea we've already considered of 'flags' in the sense of *irises* and 'the *flagging* pursuit of happiness'[42] of which those same flowers might have been emblematic. The second is the insistence on what lies behind 'the eyes just slits',[43] with its specific echo of the scene between Gretta and *Gabriel* (his name finding a near version in 'Krapp' itself) in which 'she looked away from him along the shaft of light towards the window in silence'.[44] For Krapp is the Gabriel who would 'fade and wither dismally with age',[45] still insisting on 'the fire in me now'[46] even as, in Joyce's phrase, 'his soul had approached that region where dwell the vast hosts of the dead'.[47] This 'region', located somewhere in the west of Ireland, is surely where, as Devlin has it:

> Water withers from the oars. The pilgrims blacken
> Out of the boats to masticate their sin
> Where Dante smelled among the stones and bracken
> The door to Hell.[48]

The connection between St Patrick's Purgatory and Dante, who reputedly made a pilgrimage to this isolated lake in County Donegal, would have had a particular appeal to Beckett, crouching like Belacqua at his feet, while Devlin's phrase 'to masticate their sin' surely plays on the mastication/masturbation nexus in a way that Beckett picks up on in the banana/erection of *la banane* and *La Dernière Bande*.

## Edgeworth

That's *La Dernière Bande*, 'spelt as pronounced', as Arthur advises Mr Graves (surely some relation to Alfred Perceval and his son Robert) of the spelling of the aphrodisiac 'Bando' (surely some relation) in *Watt*,

Beckett's spoof of the 'Big House' novel. The genre can be traced back to one book, *Castle Rackrent* by Maria Edgeworth (1768–1849), published anonymously in 1800, the pivotal year in Irish history to which Edgeworth alludes in her introduction:

When Ireland loses her identity by an union with Great Britain, she will look back, with a smile of good-natured complacency, on the Sir Kits and Sir Condys of her former existence.[49]

The avant-garde aspect of *Castle Rackrent*, now scarcely noticeable, is twofold. The image of territorial expansion, indeed, is used by Walter Allen, in *The English Novel*, to describe the book's first claim to fame:

Miss Edgeworth occupied new territory for the novel. Before her, except when London was the scene, the locale of our fiction had been generalized, conventionalized . . . Miss Edgeworth gave fiction a local habitation and a name. And she did more than this: she perceived the relation between the local habitation and the people who dwell in it. She invented, in other words, the regional novel[50]

The second, revolutionary aspect of the book is set down with all his customary succinctness by my old professor, John Cronin, in his study of *The Anglo-Irish Novel*:

In making [Thady Quirk] the narrator and controller of the novel's point of view, she established a new technique of fiction and presented commentators with a cat's-cradle of speculation about her central figure and the relationship between him and his material.[51]

It is this relationship between the protagonist and his or her material, including the ordering of that material, which Beckett, who had already touched on the subject in *Molloy*—'I began at the beginning—like an old ballocks—can you imagine that?'[52]—would take to its logical conclusion in *Watt*:

As Watt told the beginning of his story, not first, but second, so not fourth, but third, now he told its end. Two, one, four, three, that was the order in which Watt told his story.[53]

By the end, if such there be, of the novel, Mr Knott's big house has been transmogrified into a station waiting-room, the nave into the narthex, in which the signalman, Mr Case, is 'reading a book: "*Songs by the Way"* by George Russell (A.E.). Mr Case had a very superior taste in books, for a signal-man.'[54] In my next chapter, I'll be focusing on how a range of writers, from Ferguson through Hewitt to Joyce and Kavanagh (all of them afforded, to a greater or lesser extent, an 'edge' by Maria Edgeworth), have responded to what I've termed elsewhere the 'eternal interim' of Ireland.

# 2

## 'Such a Local Row'

# Ferguson

I'D like to concentrate here on the idea of writer as public man or woman, an idea embodied in the figure of Amergin, the poet who puts it about, if you recall, that he speaks 'for Erin'. I'll look at the strategies devised by several Irish writers who are determined to speak 'for Erin' or sometimes, just as determinedly, not. One way or another, it does seem that Irish writers again and again find themselves challenged by the violent juxtaposition of the concepts of 'Ireland' and 'I'. Irish writers have a tendency to interpose themselves between the two, like that narrow-shouldered little comma in the general title of this series of talks, either to bring them closer together, or to force them further apart. It's as if they feel obliged to extend the notion of being a 'medium' to becoming a 'mediator'.

As you know, the phrase 'To Ireland, I' is taken from the exchange between the murdered King Duncan's sons in Act II Scene iii of *Macbeth*:

MALCOLM. What will you do? Let's not consort with them.
   To show an unfelt sorrow is an office
   Which the false man does easy. I'll to England.
DONALBAIN. To Ireland, I; our separated fortune
   Shall keep us both the safer. Where we are
   There's daggers in men's smiles; the near in blood,
   The nearer bloody.[1]

On one hand, Malcolm and Donalbain realize that their lives are in danger and their first impulse is to save themselves, to find neutral ground. On the other, they're very conscious of the strategic advantages of being on neutral ground, a ground from which countermeasures may be taken.

I can't say if some version of this exchange between Malcolm and Donalbain made it into the *Macbeth* offered in *Shakespearian Breviates*, since I've not as yet been able to track down a copy of this 1882 book by Sir Samuel Ferguson (1810–86), in which Ferguson 'adjusted to convenient reading' twenty-four of the longer plays of Shakespeare. I can say that, even without looking at the book, I find myself agreeing with the following verdict by Arthur Deering in his 1931 account of *Sir Samuel Ferguson, Poet and Antiquarian*:

Ferguson, who had been reading Shakespeare since 1869, hit upon the idea of cutting these plays down to two hours' reading time. Perhaps nothing the man has done reveals quite so much of his egotism and his self-assurance. In reducing these plays to a definite time allowance, Ferguson has ruthlessly sacrificed all that motivation which is so essential to character development in the drama. The absence of motivation has been a marked characteristic of all of Ferguson's literary work.[2]

This charge by Deering (who is, by the way, the classic example of a thesis writer who tires of his subject almost as soon as he engages with it), this charge of an 'absence of motivation' is quite well founded. There's an extraordinarily dull and dutiful feel to much of the writing in Ferguson's longer poems. One finds oneself wondering if he mightn't have more effectively spent his time and energy in 'adjusting' some of his own work 'to convenient reading'. So I hope you won't mind if I do a little 'adjusting' here on his behalf, presenting you with a few snippets from Ferguson's *Poems* and his *Lays of the Western Gael*.[3] I'm not going to comment extensively on them just now, but I do assure you that I have a purpose, and will return to them later. Typical of Ferguson's tone is this extract from 'The Tain-Quest':

Wherefore from that fruitless session went I forth myself in quest
Of the Tain; nor intermission, even for hours of needful rest,
Gave I to my sleepless searches, till I Erin, hill and plain,
Courts and castles, cells and churches, roam'd and ransack'd, but in vain.

Brazen-sandall'd, vapour-shrouded, moving in an icy blast,
Through the doorway terror-crowded, up the tables Fergus pass'd:—
'Stay thy hand, oh harper, pardon! Cease the wild unearthly lay!
Murgen, bear thy sire his guerdon.' Murgen sat, a shape of clay.

In 'Conary', Ferguson gives a version of *Togail Bruidne Da Derga*, 'The Destruction of Da Derga's Hostel'. This is the story of Conaire Mor, a king who is fated to break a series of *geasa*, or taboos, and suffer a series of attacks by marauders on his hostel, situated somewhere in the environs of modern Dublin. The hostel is set on fire and the water source runs out. Conaire dies of thirst, and is then decapitated. In some versions of the story, MacCecht the 'cup-bearer', is charged by Conaire's severed head to search the length and breadth of Ireland for water. In others, the search is undertaken by Conall Carnach. In Ferguson's version, there's some sense of what he calls the *gaysh*, the taboo, but no dramatization of the cause and effect. We learn of the significance of each *gaysh* after it's been broken. Needless to say, the man who feels the need to make Shakespeare more manageable isn't going to have much truck with decapitation, though he does allude to it in a passage that stands out from the homogenized, ultra-heat-treated generality of the tale:

> 'The foremost this, the mightiest champion this
> Left of the Red Branch, since Cuchullin's fall.
> Look you, as thick as fragments are of ice
> When one night's frost is crackled underfoot,
> As thick as Autumn leaves, as blades of grass,
> Shall the lopped members and the cloven half-heads
> Of them that hear me, be, by break of day,
> Before Da-Derga's doors, if this assault
> Be given, while Conall Carnach waits within!'

This Conall Carnach, the son of the second Amairgin, is a specialist in limb-removals and beheadings. Among his many distinctions is the killing of Mesgegra and the mixing of Mesgegra's brains with lime into a calcified ball. This 'Mesgedra', as Ferguson has his name, is the subject of another *Lay*, in the introductory note to which he's typically coy about the violent subject matter of the brain-ball:

If we inquire into its nature, or ask how the trophy of a dead man could supply materials for a missile from a sling, we enter on shocking details such as deform the traditions of this as well as every other old country which has preserved its literary rudiments.

This combination of coyness and the 'absence of motivation' we remarked on earlier proves fatal. Ferguson scarcely mentions the brain-ball, the one that Cet or Ceth will fire at Connor MacNessa, the one that lodges in Connor's brain until it shakes loose on Good Friday and dies. In 'The Healing of Conall Carnach', Ferguson focuses on the magical recovery of Conall Carnach after he kills Ceth:

Over Slieve Few, with noiseless tramping through the heavy-drifted snow,
Bealcu, Connacia's champion, in his chariot tracks the foe;

And anon far off discerneth, in the mountain-hollow white,
Slinger Keth and Conall Carnach mingling, hand to hand, in fight.

Westward then through Breiffny's borders, with his captive and his dead,
Tracked by bands of fierce applauders, wives and shrieking widows, sped;
And the chain'd heroic carcass on the fair-green of Moy Slaught
Casting down, proclaim'd his purpose, and bade Lee the leech be brought.

Conall to the green well-margin came at dawn and knelt to drink,
Thinking how a noble virgin by a like green fountain's brink
Heard his own pure vows one morning far away and long ago:
All his heart to home was turning; and his tears began to flow.

And the Sun, through starry stages measuring from the Ram and Bull,
Tells us of renewing Ages, and that Nature's time is full:
So, perchance, these silly breezes even now may swell the sail,
Brings the leavening word of Jesus westward also to the Gael.

These images of 'westward' motion, 'tears' and 'heavy-drifted snow'
are prefigurings of the last paragraphs of James Joyce's 'The Dead', as
are images from another *Lay*, 'Aideen's Grave'. Ferguson sets the
scene in an introductory note for his depiction of how 'Aideen, daughter of Angus of Ben-Edar [now the Hill of Howth], died of grief for
the loss of her husband, Oscar, son of Ossian':

> Here, far from camp and chase removed,
>     Apart in Nature's quiet room,
> The music that alive she loved
>     Shall cheer her in the tomb.
>
> In sweet remembrance of the days
>     When, duteous, in the lowly vale,
> Unconscious of my Oscar's gaze,
>     She filled the fragrant pail,
>
> And, duteous, from the running brook
>     Drew water for the bath; nor deem'd
> A king did on her labour look,
>     And she a fairy seem'd.
>
> But when the wintry frosts begin,
>     And in their long drawn, lofty flight,
> The wild geese with their airy din

Distend the ear of night.

A cup of bodkin-pencill'd clay
   Holds Oscar; mighty heart and limb
One handful now of ashes grey:
   And she has died for him.

The Ogham from her pillar-stone
   In tract of time will wear away;
Her name at last be only known
   In Ossian's echo'd lay.

Let change as may the face of earth,
   Let alter all the social frame,
For mortal men the ways of birth
   And death are still the same.

Of Oscar and Aideen bereft,
   So Ossian sang. The Fenians sped
Three mighty shouts to heaven; and left
   Ben Edar to the dead.

Not only do we have the title, 'The Dead', in that last line but the central idea of 'the music that alive she loved | shall cheer her in her tomb' is carried over to the story. I've quoted at length from Ferguson partly to give some sense of what I've already hinted at—an odd combination of engagement with, and detachment from, his Irish subject matter. His engagement is, of course, comparatively extensive, extensive enough to merit his election in 1882 to the Presidency of the Royal Irish Academy. Among the subjects Ferguson addresses in essays and articles over the years are 'An Account of the Ogham Inscriptions in the Cave at Rath Croghan, County Roscommon' (we recognize this Croghan as the hill palace of Medhbh and Ailill) and 'On the Ceremonial Turn, Called Desuil'. Yet, as I say, there's such a curiously bloodless feel to his writing that it's hard to understand why Yeats, for example, might write in the Introduction to *A Book of Irish Verse* (1895) that 'Conary' was 'the best Irish poem of any kind'.[4] Writing in *The Bookman* a year later, Yeats proclaimed:

In a debate, 'Who is the National poet of Ireland?', Ferguson was voted the place held by Davis and Moore . . . Mangan had a more lyrical temperament, Allingham a more delicate ear, a more distinguished mastery over words. But

Ferguson had his roots in Irish character and Irish history. He foreshadowed the way of the poets who would come after him.[5]

By which, we may take it, Yeats means Yeats. Ferguson is, of course, one of the three poets of whom Yeats would write, 'Would that I were counted one | With Davis, Mangan, Ferguson.' I have to confess that the way the stress falls on that last syllable—Fergu*son*—always raises a little smile for me, making it hard for me to decide if Yeats was preying upon, rather than falling prey to, Ferguson's notoriously 'defective ear', as it was described by Hugh Walker in his *Literature of the Victorian Era*:

It is presumably on *Congal*, a rhymed epic in five books, that Ferguson's admirers base their claim for him. But mere bulk without inspiration counts for little. His verse is usually commonplace and often gravely defective . . . Clearly, Ferguson had a defective ear and was hardly the man to sustain himself through the long flight of an Epic.[6]

Not so, Yeats would rejoin, if we were to go by the evidence of his essay in the *Dublin University Review* of November 1886 on 'The Poetry of Sir Samuel Ferguson', when he deals with how Ferguson was received by his readers:

If Samuel Ferguson had written of Arthur and of Guinevere, they would have received him gladly: that he chose rather to tell of Congal and of desolate and queenly Deirdre, we give him full-hearted thanks; he has restored to our hills and rivers their epic interest. The nation has found in Davis a battle-call, as in Mangan its cry of despair; but he only, the one Homeric poet of our time, could give us immortal companions still wet with the dew of their primal world.

When Yeats goes on to argue that 'the author of these poems is the greatest poet Ireland had produced, because the most central and most Celtic', he cuts to the heart of the issue. The main requirement of the poet who might answer the call to rhymes and 'speak for Erin' is that his or her subject matter be Irish.

## *Giraldus Cambrensis*

I take my cue from Yeats's defining characteristic of an Irish writer as a dealer in specifically Irish subject matter when I indulge in a little rascality and include here the rascally Giraldus Cambrensis, or Gerald of Wales (c.1146–1223) whose *History and Topography of Ireland*[7] was published, in the sense of its being publicly read aloud, at Oxford in or about 1188. I have to tell you that I was somewhat alarmed, as I prepared for this talk, by Giraldus's report in *De Rebus*—he speaks of himself in the third person—of how things are done in this part of the world. 'Since his book was divided into three parts,' he writes, 'he gave three consecutive days to the reading, a part being read each day. On the first he hospitably entertained the poor of the whole town whom he had gathered together for that purpose; on the morrow he entertained all the doctors of the divers faculties, and those of their scholars who were best known and best spoken of; and on the third day he entertained the remainder of the scholars together with the knights of the town and a number of citizens. It was a magnificent and costly achievement . . . '. I have to confess that I lost my nerve and stopped reading at that point and went back, for a little light relief, to Giraldus's account of the island of Ireland and some of its strange and startling sights, an account that draws in part on *Lebor Gabála*, 'The Book of Invasions', since it gives us the familiar line about the arrival of the sons of Milesius, including Heberus and Herimon. There are accounts of the barnacle geese that 'at first appear as excrescences on fir logs'. There's an account of 'a lake in Ulster which contains an island divided into two parts'—St Patrick's Purgatory, Lough Derg, the subject of poems by both Denis Devlin and Patrick Kavanagh—and an 'island in the sea west of Connacht in which human corpses are not buried and do not putrefy, but are placed in the open and remain without corruption'. For the most part, Giraldus is quite determined to amass as much evidence as possible to substantiate the idea that the Irish 'are a wild and inhospitable people. They live on beasts only, and live like beasts.' He is, after all, the most public of writers, a political propagandist.

## Goldsmith

Another less likely political propagandist is Oliver Goldsmith (1728–74), whose early experience of life on a farm near Ballymahon, in Westmeath, informs his picture of Auburn, 'The Deserted Village' of his most famous poem:

> But now the sounds of population fail,
> No cheerful murmurs fluctuate in the gale,
> No busy steps the grass-grown footway tread,
> For all the bloomy flush of life is fled;
> All but yon widowed, solitary thing
> That feebly bends beside the plashy spring;
> She, wretched matron, forced in age, for bread,
> To strip the brook with mantling cresses spread,
> To pick her wintry faggot from the thorn,
> To seek her nightly shed and weep till morn;
> She only left of all the harmless train,
> The sad historian of the pensive plain.

Now, it's clear from the wider context that Auburn is not an Irish town. Though much of the blame for its demise goes back to the English Enclosure Acts, it's not exactly an English town, either. Part of the difficulty with the poem is its very non-specificity of locale. It's as if Goldsmith has decided that neither England nor Ireland is to be favoured. There's a clue, I think, both to the Irish provenance of the village and Goldsmith's immediate resistance to it in the one instance of wobbly prosody in these iambic pentameters—'No cheerful murmurs fluctuate in the gale'. One might argue, I suppose, that the 'fluctuate' is mimetic of what it describes. The trouble is that, despite his best efforts, this infelicity draws even more attention to a reading Goldsmith wants to conceal or counter—'No cheerful murmurs *fluctuate* in the *Gael*', as in Sir Samuel Ferguson's 'Western Gael'.


# Graves

Or the Gael in *Songs of the Gael*, a collection published in 1925 by Alfred Perceval Graves (1846–1931), father of Robert Graves. It was Graves who had asked the question, 'Has Ireland a National Poet?', alluded to by Yeats in his 1896 piece for *The Bookman*. 'We do not use the term national in the sense of belonging to the Nationalist party in Ireland,' Graves had reflected, with cunning circumspection, in his 1888 essay in *The Reflector*, 'We wished to make use of our word national, as distinguished from Nationalist, clear from the outset'.[8] This distinction, and Graves's sense that he needs to announce it, sets up in a word or two a supreme difficulty facing the Irish writer. Can he or she adequately reflect the complexity of the Irish political situation *without* becoming a propagandist? Graves goes on to give three main reasons for Ferguson, again, having 'reached heights hitherto unattained by any Irish poetical writer— heights which justly entitle him to rank as the national poet of Ireland'. To begin with, there's his apolitical nature, the fact that he is 'a Belfast man of a fine old Presbyterian stock who, marvellous to relate, has had the sense to eschew politics in verse'. What is being applauded here seems to have more to do with civic, or civil, than literary concerns. Then there's the fact that 'the country has at last found a poet who can worthily express the national character in its noblest aspects—aspects which Ireland has, alas! latterly only too often lost sight of '. This idea of a 'national character' and 'its noblest aspects' probably wouldn't include headhunting or brain-balling or such pastimes and pursuits. The third main reason is his 'virile . . . vision' of his subject matter:

The terrible shapes of Celtic superstition—the Giant Walker, the Washer of the Ford—loom monstrously before us as he sings, and he marshals the contending hosts at Moyra with a magnificent realism to which we know no modern parallel.[9]

No modern parallel, maybe, but Yeats was not alone in drawing comparisons between Ferguson and the ancients when he described him, if you recall, as 'the one Homeric poet of our time'. Yeats's exorbitant praise of Ferguson appeared, as I mentioned, in *The Dublin University Review* of November 1886, three months after Ferguson's death, and includes, as R. F. Foster describes it in *W. B. Yeats: A Life*, a passage in which he 'thumbed the nose both at Sligo and Dowden',[10] by which he means both the Anglo-Irish middle class from which he sprang and Edward Dowden, the professor at Trinity College, Dublin, who was a well-known opponent of Home Rule:

I do not appeal to the professional classes, who, in Ireland, at least, appear at no time to have thought of the affairs of their country till they first feared for their emolument—nor do I appeal to the shoddy society of 'West Briton-ism'—but to those young men clustered here and there throughout our land, whom the emotion of Patriotism has lifted into that world of selfless passion in which heroic deeds are possible and heroic poetry possible.[11]

Yeats allows for something of a reassessment ten years later when, in the course of his *Bookman* review of Lady Ferguson's *Sir Samuel Ferguson in the Ireland of his Day*, from which I quoted earlier, he concludes that

Ferguson lived among the professional condemnors of the multitude . . . Heaviness crept into his rhythm and his language. This marred the barbaric power of *Conary* (still the most characteristic of his Irish poems), and made the Homeric imagination of *Congal* without avail.[12]

# Lady Gregory

In August 1896, only months after he delivered himself of that assess-ment, Yeats met Augusta Gregory (1852–1932), whom he encouraged in her collection of folk tales and legends. In his introduction to her *Gods and Fighting Men* (1904), he writes:

It has been said, and I think the Japanese were the first to say it, that the four essential virtues are to be generous among the weak, and truthful among one's friends, and brave among one's enemies, and courteous at all times . . . Companionship can only be perfect when it is founded on things, for things are always the same under the hand, and at last one comes to hear with envy the voices of boys lighting a lantern to ensnare moths, or of the maids chat-tering in the kitchen about the fox that carried off a turkey before breakfast. Lady Gregory's book of tales is full of fellowship untroubled like theirs, and made noble by a courtesy that has gone perhaps out of the world.[13]

Among the tales Lady Gregory includes are a series having to do with the coming of the Gael. Among the incidents touched upon is the meeting by Amergin of a beautiful woman who announces herself to be Banba, wife of Mac Cuill, Son of the Hazel. There are two other queens, Fodhla, wife of Mac Cecht, Son of the Plow, and Ériu, wife of Mac Gréinne, Son of the Sun. This last sometimes takes the form of a sharp-beaked, grey-white crow, not unlike the Morrigu, the bird of battle who taunts the youthful Cuchulainn:

'There is not the making of a hero in you,' she said to him, 'and you lying there under the feet of shadows.' And with that Cuchulainn rose up and struck off the head of a shadow that was standing over him, with his hurling stick.

One of the enchantments wrought by the Tuatha De Danaan, 'that never change and that never die', on the Gael as they attempt to land near Inver Sceine and take control of the country involves a treacherous wave on account of which 'Ir, son of Miled, came to his death . . . and his body was cast on the shore, and it is buried in a small island that is called Sceilg Michill.' There's the story of Aoibhell, a fairy woman who falls in love with a young man of Munster, Dubhlaing ua Artigan, and tries to help him in fighting on behalf of the Gael by putting what she calls a 'Druid covering about him, the way no one could see him'. Dubhlaing ua Artigan refuses to save himself and dies in the battle of Clontarf. Lady Gregory also recounts the story of Da Derga's Inn and 'the night Conaire, the High King of Ireland, met with his death', including a reference to those *geasa*, or taboos. There are the three sons of Lugaidh Menn, another king of Ireland, Eochaid, whose 'house was never without music or drinking of ale', Fiacha who 'never said a word too much', and Ruide, who 'never refused any one, and never asked anything at all of any man'. There's the tale of Áine, 'that some say was the Morrigu herself', and the vengeance she took on Oilioll, a king of Ireland who killed her brother:

She made a great yew-tree by enchantment beside the river Maigh in Luimnech, and she put a little man in it, playing sweet music on a harp. And Oilioll's son was passing the river with his step-brother, and they saw the tree and heard the sweet music from it. And first they quarrelled as to which of them would have the little harper, and then they quarrelled about the tree, and they asked a judgement from Oilioll, and he gave it for his own son. And it was bad feeling about that judgement that led to the battle of Mucruimhe, and Oilioll and his seven sons were killed there, and so Aine got her revenge.[14]

## Hewitt

I'm going to turn for a moment from that local row at Mucruimhe to comment on the conceit of man in, or as, tree, an idea that I've touched on already in the use of the word 'stock', the trunk or stem of a tree, in the phrase I quoted from Alfred Perceval Graves's description of Ferguson as 'a Belfast man of a fine old Presbyterian stock'. This conceit is central to the work of John Hewitt (1907–87), a Belfast man of fine old Methodist stock, whose poetry is much concerned with the grafting of one culture upon the stock of another, with the putting down of roots by one group coinciding with the de*rac*ination or ex*tirp*ation of another, with the impact of the *Plantation* of Ulster on what the speaker of one of his poems describes as 'the barbarian tribesmen'[15] whom they've 'smoked out' by having 'felled the trees'. (We might remember that the word for a tree in Irish is *crann*, so that Elizabeth Bowen's naming of her doomed Anglo-Irish dynasty in her short story 'The Tommy Crans' has a further 'Erinic' overlay.) The Hewitt poem I've just quoted is one of his best known, 'The Colony', in which the speaker is a Roman who describes how 'when they'd surveyed the land . . . we planted little towns to garrison | the heaving country'. The speaker through whom Hewitt throws his voice concludes that colonizer and colonist have much in common:

> the rain against the lips, the changing light,
> the heavy clay-sucked stride, have altered us;
> we would be strangers in the Capitol;
> this is our country also, no-where else;
> and we shall not be outcast on the world.

Astonishingly, 'The Colony' was written in 1950. Despite its tonal inconsistencies ('bade' and 'I have a harder row to hoe' don't sit happily together) and the 'heavy clay-sucked stride' of its iambics (shades of Ferguson's 'defective ear') it remains a powerful political poem. I speak of Hewitt 'throwing his voice' through a Roman, a technique we think of as Browningesque, with its 'in character' asides such as, of the natives, 'Also they breed like flies. The danger's there.' The dramatic monologue allows Hewitt to say what would otherwise be unsaid, or unsayable, in polite society. The same is true of what I think is Ferguson's least typical, and best, poem, 'At the Polo Ground', or 'In Carey's Footsteps', which was published not in his collected poems but in Lady Ferguson's *Sir Samuel Ferguson in the Ireland of His Day*. Here Ferguson presents a character who is psychologically verifiable and, to go back to Deering's term, 'motivated'. For the character he so daringly ventriloquizes is James Carey, a leader of the 'Invincibles', the hard-line group of Fenians who, on 6 May 1882, assassinated the chief secretary of Ireland, Lord Frederick Cavendish, and an under-secretary in Dublin Castle, Thomas Henry Burke. Carey gave the signal for the attack while attending a polo-match in Phoenix Park:

> Here I am
> Behind the hurdles fencing off the ground
> They've taken from us who have a right to it,
> For these select young gentry and their sport.
> Curse them! I would they all might break their necks!
> Young fops and lordlings of the garrison
> Kept up by England here to keep us down.

'Kept *up* by England here to keep us *down*?' Is this the same Sir Samuel Ferguson we all knew and couldn't quite bring ourselves to love? Surely not. This one continues with uncustomary deftness and delicacy and deliberation and something approaching delight:

> Up. Drive on straight,—if I blow my nose
> And show my handkerchief in front of them,
> And then turn back, what's that to anyone?
> No further, driver. Back to Island Bridge.
> No haste. If some acquaintance chanced to pass,
> He must not think that we are running away.
> I don't like, but I can't help looking back.
> They meet: my villains pass them. Gracious Powers,
> Another failure! No, they turn again
> And overtake; and Brady lifts his arm—
> I'll see no more. On—by the Monument.
> On—brisker, brisker—but yet leisurely.
> By this time all is over with them both.
> Ten minutes more, the Castle has the news,
> And haughty Downing Street in half an hour
> Is struck with palsy.[16]

Despite a slight wobble in that editorializing 'villains', and the all-Browning tone (the poem was written, it seems, as an exercise to show how easily Browning could be imitated), Ferguson's engagement here

with his subject matter is all out. The matter-of-fact, throwaway style
is perfectly judged to the end:

> Still in time
> To catch the tram, I'll take a seat a-top—
> For no one must suppose I've anything
> To hide—and show myself in Grafton Street.[17]


## Hyde

The phrase 'anything | To hide' brings me neatly to the case of
Douglas Hyde (1860–1949), the title of whose inaugural address to the
National Literary Society on 25 November 1892 suggests that he was a
man intent on making his case quite forthrightly. The talk is called
quite simply 'On the Necessity for De-Anglicizing Ireland':

If we take a bird's-eye view of our island today, and compare it with what it
used to be, we must be struck by the extraordinary fact that the nation which
was once, as every one admits, one of the most classically learned and cultured
nations in Europe, is now one of the least so; how one of the most reading and
literary peoples has become one of the *least* studious and most *un*-literary, and
how the present art products of one of the quickest, most sensitive, and most
artistic races on earth are now only distinguished for their hideousness.[18]

Most 'hideous', Hyde argues, is the loss of the language:

I have no hesitation at all in saying that every Irish-feeling Irishman, who
hates the reproach of West-Britonism, should set himself to encourage the
efforts which are being made to keep alive our once great national tongue.[19]

This contrasting of a glorious 'then' with a grimy 'now' (as with AE's
peasant 'Exiles' in whom 'Through the swarthy faces | The starry
faces shine'), is a central element in the rhetoric of late nineteenth-
century cultural nationalism. I give, by way of example, a few key sentences from Standish O'Grady's great *History of Ireland: Critical and
Philosophical* (1881):

From a time dating for more than three thousand years before the birth of
Christ, the stream of Hibernian history flows down interrupted, copious and
abounding . . . to think that this mighty fabric of recorded events, so stupendous

in its dimensions, so clean and accurate in its details, so symmetrical and elegant, should be after all a mirage and delusion, a gorgeous bubble, whose glowing rotundity, whose rich hues, azure, purple, amethyst and gold, vanish at a touch and are gone, leaving a sorry remnant over which the patriot disillusioned may grieve . . . Running down the long list of Milesian kings, chiefs, brehons and bards, where first shall we pause, arrested by some substantial form in this procession of empty ghosts—how distinguish the man from the shadow, when over all is diffused the same concealing mist, and the eyes of the living and the dead look with the same pale glare?[20]

The great sweep and swagger of O'Grady's prose is pursued by Hyde, in whom you will recognize some of the images I've concentrated on here:

It may be said, roughly speaking, that the ancient Gaelic civilisation died with O'Connell, largely, I am afraid, owing to his example and his neglect of inculcating the necessity of keeping alive racial customs, language, and traditions . . . Thomas Davis and his brilliant band of Young Irelanders came just at the dividing of the line, and tried to give to Ireland a new literature in English to replace the literature which was just being discarded. It succeeded and it did not succeed. It was a most brilliant effort, but the old bark had been too recently stripped off the Irish tree, and the trunk could not take as it might have done to a fresh one.

We recognize Hyde's grafting metaphor, though it seems a little confused here in terms of whether it's 'trunk' or 'slip' that 'takes'. We recognize, also, the liminal/narthecal position of the Young Irelanders 'just at the dividing of the line'. Having appealed to the past, Hyde will shortly appeal to the future vis-à-vis the Irish language:

To a person taking a bird's-eye-view of the situation a hundred or five hundred years hence, believe me, it will also appear of greater importance than any mere temporary wrangle, but, unhappily, our countrymen cannot be brought to see this.

## Irwin

On the subject of the 'mere temporary wrangle' between himself and his next-door neighbour, Thomas Caulfield Irwin (1823–92), I'll allow a certain John O'Donovan a word or two:

He says I am his enemy, and watch him through the thickness of the wall which divides our houses. One of us must leave. I have a houseful of books; he has an umbrella and a revolver.[21]

Irwin's idea that John O'Donovan could see through walls is particularly amusing when one thinks that this is the one and same O'Donovan who, between 1834 and 1841, was involved in the Ordnance Survey of Ireland, a task involving every conceivable manner of delineation and demarcation, not only in topographical matters, but matters of folklore and linguistics. Between 1836 and 1840, O'Donovan helped catalogue the holdings of Irish manuscripts at Trinity College, Dublin. He later edited a number of texts for the Irish Archaeological Society, including *The Banquet of Dunagay and the Battle of Moira* (1842), which (you've guessed it) his friend Sir Samuel Ferguson used as a template for *Congal*.

# Joyce

One could be forgiven for thinking that all of Irish, and indeed, almost all of world literature had been produced merely as a *reamh sceal*, a prelude or preliminary piece, to the work of the greatest of all Irish writers, James Joyce (1882–1941). I want to suggest, though, that Ferguson's *Congal*, as well as a number of the other texts I've already mentioned here, are significant feeder-springs into the great reservoir of Joyce's short story 'The Dead', a story on which I've already touched in my discussions of Beckett and Bowen. I'll be concentrating here on its political aspect, what I see as its critique of late nineteenth-century Irish cultural nationalism. 'The Dead' was written in 1907. It is the last story in the carefully plotted *Dubliners*.[22] Joyce is famously on record as saying of this book that

My intention was to write a chapter of the moral history of my country and I chose Dublin for the scene because that city seemed to me the centre of paralysis. I have tried to present it to the indifferent public under four of its aspects: childhood, adolescence, maturity, and public life. The stories are arranged in this order.[23]

This *public* aspect of 'The Dead' is almost entirely overlooked, so far as I can see, and understandably so, perhaps, since the story seems to focus primarily on a very private party, in the Dublin house of Kate and Julia Morkan, sometime in early January 1904, perhaps even 6 January, Twelfth Night, the Feast of the Epiphany. Among the guests are the main characters of the story, Gabriel Conroy and his wife, Gretta, who have come in on this snowy night from the suburb of Monkstown, though they plan, strangely, to stay overnight at the Gresham Hotel. Other guests include Mary Jane, a niece of the Morkans and a music student; Freddy Malins, a drunk; Mr Browne, a Protestant; and Miss Ivors, 'a frank-mannered talkative young woman', as the narrator of the story describes her, with whom Gabriel finds himself partnered in lancers:

She did not wear a low-cut bodice and the large brooch which was fixed in the front of her collar bore on it an Irish device. When they had taken their places she said abruptly:—I have a crow to pluck with you.

This last phrase about plucking a 'crow' is used by John Kelleher in his magnificently provocative 1964 essay, 'Irish History and Mythology in James Joyce's "The Dead" ',[24] as one of several pieces of persuasive evidence that a significant strain of 'The Dead' may be drawn from that Old Irish saga *Togail Bruidne Da Derga*, 'The Destruction of Da Derga's Hostel'. This, as we already know from Ferguson, is the story of Conaire Mor, the king whom Kelleher identifies as 'Conroy' from the fact that Gabriel smiles 'at the three syllables' Lily, the caretaker's daughter, 'had given his surname'. Conaire Mor breaks a series of *geasa*, or taboos, one having to do with going right-hand-wise, or *desiul*, round Tara. Kelleher points out that Gabriel Conroy would have had Tara Street on his right on the way in from Monkstown. Another *geas* has to do with 'three reds shall not go before thee to Red's House', which Kelleher relates to three instances of 'redness', in clothing and faces, before Gabriel and Gretta arrive at the Gresham which, he argues, 'would suit admirably as a surrogate Da Derga's hostel', what with its 'red brick'. Yet another *geas* has to do with hunting birds, since Conaire's father had come to his mother in the shape of a bird. At one point in the story, Kelleher reminds us, Gabriel announces that he stands 'ready to carve a flock of geese, if necessary' while, as I mentioned earlier, 'there are Miss Ivors' ominous first words to him, "I have a crow to pluck with you." ' However persuasive John Kelleher might be here, he misses several points that would make his argument even more forceful. He might have noticed the version of 'Dodder', the river on which the hostel was supposedly built, as well as a version of the hostel itself, in the phrase 'Aunt Kate came *toddling* out of the *supper-room*'.[25] The raiders who attack the hostel, the brigands, appear in the place name 'Ball*briggan*', where Gabriel Conroy's brother is 'now senior curate'.[26] But to pursue John Kelleher in a more substantial and engaging way, as he has been pursued engagingly and substantially by both Stanley Sultan[27] and Maria Tymoczko,[28] I look first of all to his comments on the bird imagery drawn from *Togail Bruidne Da Derga*. Kelleher misses a telling circumlocution towards the end of the story when Browne exhorts his cab-driver to 'Make like a bird for Trinity College.' (Browne, by the way, particularly in the Hiberno-Norman form, de Brun, would be a close approximation of the pronunciation of *Bruidne* in *Togail Bruidne Da Derga*.) Browne's unspoken, underlying subtext is to go not so much 'fast as a bird' but 'as the crow flies'. Joyce resists an overt mention of 'crow', partly because of Miss Ivors's already having 'a crow to pluck with you'. This 'crow' is surely a manifestation of the Morrigu, or Morrigan, the bird of battle whose name finds its way directly into 'The Dead' as 'Morkan', the family name that presides over all, and the adjective 'murky' used of the 'murky morning sky'. The Morrigan also appears almost invisibly as 'Mary Jane'. Kelleher might also have noticed that, with respect to the *geas*, Gretta's ghost lover, Michael Furey, is described as being 'in the *gas*works', a phrase Joyce uses twice, in consecutive sentences, drawing so much attention to it as to suggest that Joyce himself is 'in the *geas*works', in the business of attending to those *geasa*. At one point in the evening, Gabriel notices how 'the flame of the *gas* lit up the rich bronze' of Gretta's hair. The bird-*geas* or taboo is rendered, moreover, in the word 'geese', a word for which Joyce has a special regard, since the 'barnacle' of his wife's name, Nora Barnacle, is a barnacle *goose*, a beast whose provenance you'll recall from Giraldus Cambrensis. The fact that a barnacle goose could be construed as being more barnacle than goose allowed Catholics to eat it on Friday, so circumventing the *geas*works. Now, lest you think I'm indulging here in no more than a little *guess*work, let me say first of all why I think Kelleher doesn't pursue his point. It has partly to do with his dating of the story, which he places in 1892. As Don Gifford makes clear, in his *Joyce Annotated*, the story must in fact be set after November 1903 'since Pope Pius X's *Motu Proprio* is a topic for heated discussion'.[29] It's also set after New Year, because Freddie Malins has taken 'the pledge on New Year's Eve'.[30] This later dating would have allowed Kelleher to expand the possible sources for 'The Dead' beyond what was published prior to 1892, and would, indeed, have given more weight to his suggestion that the main source for 'The Destruction of Da Derga's Hostel' was 'Whitley Strokes's edition and translation as it appeared in *Revue Celtique* in 1901 and 1902, around which time, as Stanislaus tells us in *My Brother's Keeper*, Joyce studied Irish "for a year or two" '.[31] Again, I want to suggest that Joyce's main sense of this tale comes not only from Stokes but from Ferguson, not only the Ferguson of *Conary*, but the Ferguson of the extended *Lays of the Western Gael*, which were of course available in Kelleher's favoured 1892. To begin with *Conary*. Those lines I quoted earlier about 'the lopped members and the cloven half-heads' being 'thick as fragments are of ice | When one night's frost is crackled underfoot' are reminiscent of the 'vast hosts of the dead' indivisible from the 'snow general over Ireland' at the end of the story. There's a detail, too, in Ferguson's *Conary* that helps make sense of an otherwise unintelligible passage in 'The Dead', in which Gabriel looks at Gretta and remembers 'moments of their secret life together':

He was standing with her in the cold, looking in through a grated window at a man making bottles in a roaring furnace. It was very cold. Her face, fragrant in the cold air, was quite close to his; and suddenly she called out to the man at the furnace:—Is the fire hot, sir?

This scene of extraordinary banality, with its three 'colds' followed by a 'hot' is indeed a moment of a 'secret life' derived, I think, from Ferguson's description of the bursting out of the hostel by Conall Carnach,

> And issuing, as a jet of smoke and flame
> Bursts from a fresh replenished furnace-mouth,
> He and his cohort sallied.

Another of those 'moments of their secret life together' presents an image of a 'heliotrope envelope . . . lying beside his breakfast cup'. This 'heliotrope' is less relevant for its colour than its 'turning with the sun', relating it to the term 'deshiul'. We know that Joyce sets 'Deshil' as the first word of 'The Oxen of the Sun' chapter of *Ulysses*,[32] and I want to suggest here that, already in 'The Dead', Joyce is incorporating the notion of Viconian circular movement in the image of Patrick Morkan's horse going round and round the statue of King William, as an image of political paralysis. (Bruno is also here, by the way, in the 'opposite' figure of *Browne*.) This circular motion is drawn, though, from an extended sense of the work of Ferguson, including his essay 'On the Ceremonial Turn, Called Desiul', even his sense of the route taken by James Carey in his cab past the Wellington monument in Phoenix Park with, if you recall, the notion that Downing Street is 'struck with palsy', is mimicked in the Conroys' route in 'The Dead'. There's another sense of paralysis connected with 'the flame of the gas' in which an increasingly 'tired' Gabriel admires Gretta's hair, the sense of the *cess noínden Ulad*, commonly translated as 'the nine-day debility of the Ulidians'. This 'debility' is the result of Cruinniuc Mac Agnomain's insistence that his wife, Macha, run a race against a horse while she's pregnant with twins. She wins the race, gives birth, but curses the men of Ulster that they suffer the weakness of a woman in childbirth when they're faced by danger. It's the subject of 'The Twins of Macha', another of the *Lays of the Western Gael*:

> Whence Emain Macha? And the pangs intense
> That long were wont to plague the Ultonians, whence?

I suspect that Joyce was delighted to see that Macha's husband's name is Agnomain, a ready-made near 'gnomon', which is, as we know, precisely what Gabriel turns into as the evening progresses: 'Instinctively he turned his back more to the light lest she might see the shame that burned upon his forehead'. I'm pretty sure that Tom and Eva, the Conroy children, are twins. That each story in *Dubliners* should appeal to the three elements of 'paralysis', 'gnomon' and 'simony', as announced in 'The Sisters', and that the collection as a whole be structured on 'child-hood, adolescence, maturity and public life' is reminiscent of Ferguson's architectural ambitions for *Congal* with its 'argument' set down by Ferguson in the memorably dreadful couplet:

> Ambition, Anger, Terror, Strife and Death,
> Each, here, its book in Congal's story hath.

In a note in *Congal*, to which Ferguson appends 'The Twins of Macha', he offers another reading of the etymology of the word Emain. Rather than deriving from *emain*, a twin-birth, it might derive from *eo-muin*, a phrase Ferguson translates as 'neck-bodkin'.[33] I want to pro-pose that this is a version of the brooch, with its 'Irish device' that Miss Ivors has pinned to her collar—Miss Ivors who 'did not wear a low-cut *bodice*'. But the word 'bodkin' has another force for Joyce, of course, since it's the name of the man upon whom the character of Michael Furey is based, the man with whom Nora Barnacle had been 'great' in Galway. We've already come upon his name, as I think Joyce must have, in 'Aideen's Grave', in that extraordinary phrase 'a cup of *bodkin*-pencill'd clay | Holds Oscar'. This comes, if you recall, in the midst of a poem that refers to how Aideen 'a faery seemed', faery being a near 'Furey', and insists that 'for mortal men the ways of birth | And death are still the same'. The complete stanza reads, again:

> A cup of bodkin-pencill'd clay
>     Holds Oscar; mighty heart and limb
> One handful now of ashes grey:
>     And she had died for him.

That phrase 'She had died for him' seems remarkably close to Gretta's musing of Michael Furey, 'I think he died for me'. I want to suggest, furthermore, that Joyce's sense of the extended range of Ferguson was itself extensive. The paralysed 'Morkans' are reminiscent of 'Murgen' who 'sat, a shape of clay', at the very end of 'The Tain-Quest'. The debate about the 'purest tenor voice' that dominates the dinner-table discussion is a version of the question 'Who is the national poet of Ireland?' as raised by Sir Alfred Perceval Graves. The answer to the question is 'Parkinson', a name structurally similar to 'Ferguson'. But, as I say, Joyce extends his range of reference, in a technique I think of as 'conglomewriting', to include Alfred Perceval Graves himself, who makes a discreet appearance in 'The Dead' at the grave of Michael Furey, the bed-grave in which Gretta and Gabriel settle down for the night and, more importantly perhaps, by way of allusion to his poem 'Song of the Ghost', in which a woman is visited by the spirit of her lover:

> 'My own true lover,
>   So tall and brave,
> Lives exiled over
>   The angry wave.'
> 'Your true love's body
>   Lies on the bier,
> His faithful spirit
>   Is with you here.'[34]

This poem by Graves is included in Yeats's 1888 collection of *Fairy and Folk Tales of Ireland*, which includes also Standish O'Grady's 'The Knighting of Cuchulainn', with its tale of how Cuchulainn is presented 'with his weapons of war, after he had taken the vows of the Red Branch, and having also bound himself by certain gaesa'.[35] In a footnote, the editor asserts with all his customary high- and offhandedness that these *gaesa* are 'curious vows taken by the ancient warriors. Hardly anything definite is known of them'. Yeats may not have known anything definite about *gaesa*, but Joyce surely did. Joyce also takes the 'mare, grey almost to whiteness' belonging to Macha that's hitched to a 'great car' that 'brayed and shrieked' from which Cuchulainn 'brandished his spears' and reconfigures them. First of all, there's the comment from Miss O'Callaghan on the ride home with Gabriel and Gretta in the 'old rattling box' of the cab. 'They say you never cross O'Connell Bridge,' she says, 'without seeing a white horse'. The 'vast hosts of the dead' are quite specifically associated with horses in the phrase 'the solid world itself which these dead had one time *reared* and lived in was dissolving and dwindling' while the snow that is militaristically 'general' drifts 'on the *spears* of the little gate, on the barren thorns'. This last 'thorns' reinforces the 'fairy' aspect of Furey since the idea of 'The Fairy Thorn', also the subject of a Ferguson poem, is perhaps the most common manifestation of faery, one that still carried some weight when I was a child. Let me turn now to look in closer detail at this figure of Furey, of whom Gretta is reminded by the song 'The Lass of Aughrim'. This singing marks the beginning of the conventional *féth fiada*. This is substantiated by Joyce's unconventional word choice in describing Gretta's voice, as she speaks of Michael Furey, as '*veiled* and sad'. This idea of a partition is, of course, central to the convention. So, too, is the appearance of a deer. That deer is here, in a 'veiled' way, in Furey's name, which could be rendered as *fiadh ruadh* or *fiadhradh* or *fiara*, a 'deer' or 'roebuck'. Joyce would have been familiar with this idea, if only from the 'Druid covering' in the story of Aoibhell and Dubhlaing ua Artigan in Lady Gregory's *Gods and Fighting Men*. I have a theory, which I won't advance too strongly, that the name *Dubh*laing ua *Arti*gan influences the naming of Bartell D'Arcy. I'm on slightly safer ground, I suspect, when I propose that the man who dies for love of Aoibhell ghosts the ghostly Michael Furey, and that he's mediated through Lady Gregory. We should perhaps remind ourselves of the enchanting words of the *ceo sídhe* sung by Bartell D'Arcy, himself a Morrigan or Macha figure ('Can't you see that I'm as hoarse as a *crow?*'):

> O, the rain falls on my heavy locks
> And the dew wets my skin,
> My babe lies cold . . .

This is as far as Bartell goes, as much as Joyce quotes. He resists continuing with the lines 'My babe lies cold in my arms: Lord Gregory let me in' because he resists a direct reference not so much to Lord as to *Lady* Gregory. We might bear in mind that Joyce had reviewed Lady Gregory's *Poets and Dreamers* in the *Daily Express* in March 1903, a review which he himself described in a letter to his mother as 'very severe'.[36] (James Joyce was identified as the author of that review by his initials, just as Gabriel Conroy is identified as the author of a review in that same paper by his.) Although 'The Dead' was written partly in response to the 'Playboy' riots early in 1907 in which Lady

Gregory played a leading role, Joyce does not want her name to be immediately summoned up for the reader, since it brings with it much too much cultural impedimenta of a very specific historical moment. But Lady Gregory is a presence here, however spectral, not only in the range of allusions to *Gods and Fighting Men* I've already touched on but in several others. One tale in particular, 'Midhir and Etain', might be seen as a template for the Gretta/Michael Furey story, since it deals with the love of Midhir for his supernatural lover, Etain, and the jealousy of his wife, Fuamach. Fuamach has a druid put a spell on Etain in which Angus, son of the Dagda, 'made a sunny house for her, and put sweet-smelling flowers in it, and he made invisible walls about it, that no one could see through and that could not be seen'. This version of a *féth fiada* corresponds to Furey's presence beyond the window that 'was so wet I couldn't see'. The word *fuamach* translates as 'noisy' or, one might say, 'full of sound and fury'. Etain has a daughter, Etain Og, who is bathing one day 'in the bay at Inver Cechmaine' when Midhir appears to her wearing a 'brooch of gold that reached across to his shoulders on each side'. This place name, 'Inver', prefigures Miss *Ivors* and her 'brooch which was fixed in the front of her collar'. Etain Og is later seen by the King of Ireland, Eochaid, with 'the sunlight falling on her . . . letting down her hair to wash it, and her arms out through the sleeve-holes of her shift'. This prepares the way not only for Gretta's hair—'the washing had made it fine and brilliant'—but what I call a crypto-current having to do with that word 'shift', the use of which by Synge in *The Playboy of the Western World* was one of the reasons for the aforementioned riots. Joyce is at particular pains to point out, if you recall, that Miss Ivors 'did *not* wear a low-cut bodice', while his description of the aftermath of Gretta's hairwashing lingers over the unnamed 'shift':

Perhaps she had not told him all the story. His eyes moved to the chair over which she had thrown some of her clothes. A petticoat string dangled to the floor. One boot stood upright, its limp upper fallen down: the fellow of it lay upon its side. He wondered at his riot of emotions of an hour before.[37]

This seems to me to be an extraordinarily effective fusion of the public and the private, the 'Playboy' *riot* and the '*riot* of emotions' (I'll return to the cliché shortly) of a sexually jealous man. This scenario between King Eochaid and Etain is further significant, as described by Lady Gregory, in that it's because of an attack on Midhir and his people by Eochaid that 'they brought Conaire, High King of Ireland, that was grandson of Eochaid and of Etain, to his death afterwards at Da Derga's Inn'.[38] We've already met Etain, of course, as the *Aideen* of 'Aideen's Grave'. Another word or two on Ferguson's Conary and Conall Carcach. You might recall, from 'The Healing of Conall Carnach' and 'Mesgedra', those delicate matters of headhunting and the brain-ball. These, too, find their way into 'The Dead'. 'The confusion grew greater,' Joyce writes, 'and the cabman was directed differently by Freddy Malins and Mr Browne, *each of whom had his head out through a window of the cab.*'[39] Gabriel, meanwhile, muses on his mother: 'It was strange that his mother had no musical talent, though Aunt Kate used to call her *the brains carrier* of the Morkan family'.[40] It's tempting, moreover, to think that 'Aunt Kate' is a version of MacCecht, or Keth, the 'cup-bearer', though that role is shared by her and her sister ('Aunt Kate and Aunt Julia opened and carried across from the piano bottles of stout and ale for the gentlemen and bottles of minerals for the ladies')[41] and Gabriel himself. Gabriel is, after all, named after a mediator, an emissary, a bearer of news, including news about the birth of the to-be-beheaded John the Baptist. Gabriel's speech is prefaced by Aunt Julia inviting 'all the guests to have either port or sherry' so that all present, including a reluctant Bartell D'Arcy, have their glasses filled. In this sense, Gabriel occasions, if not the bearing of a cup, the butling of a bottle or two. Which brings me back to that butler of butlers. For Gabriel's speech is surely constructed along the lines of Yeats's introduction to *Gods and Fighting Men*, with its stress on the virtues of 'fellowship' and 'a courtesy that has gone perhaps out of the world', which Gabriel echoes in 'the spirit of good *fellowship*' and 'the tradition of warm-hearted *courteous* Irish hospitality, which our forefathers have handed down to us and which we in turn hand down to our descendants'. Gabriel fears 'that this new generation . . . will lack those qualities of humanity, of hospitality, of kindly humour which belonged to an older day'.[42] This rhetorical trope is familiar to us also from Hyde's 'On the Necessity for De-Anglicizing Ireland', with its image of 'a bird's-eye view' of things in which 'the nation that once was' is set against the present 'hideousness'. The 'bird's-eye view' is more than reminiscent of the panoramic 'general' view of Ireland with which 'The Dead' ends. I want to suggest that Joyce con-glomewrites this with Standish O'Grady's 'procession of empty ghosts' and the 'mist' in which 'the eyes of the living and the dead look with the same pale glare'. It seems to me that the last phrase of the story, 'the living and the dead', comes directly from that passage in O'Grady's *History of Ireland*, particularly when it's followed in the next paragraph by a description of how 'we see duns snow-white with roofs striped crimson . . . the lively-hearted, resolute steeds . . . bearing the warrior and his charioteer with the loud clangour of rattling spears and darts' while two paragraphs later we find the image of 'flakes of fleeting and uncertain light wander and vanish; vague shapes of float-ing mist . . . vapours that conceal the solid face of nature . . . holding between us and the landscape a concealing veil' and, three paragraphs later, this:

In that dim twilight region, where day meets night, the intellect of man, tired by contact with the vulgarity of actual things, goes back for rest and recuper-ation, and there sleeping, projects its dreams against the waning night and before the rising of the sun.[43]

The 'dim twilight region' is the '*region* where dwell the hosts of the dead' in which the '*solid* world itself . . . was dissolving and dwindling' and Gabriel watches the '*flakes*, silver and dark, fall obliquely' through 'the partial darkness' in which he 'imagined he saw the form of a young man standing under a dripping tree'. Another word or two about this young man and his tree. The tree is a yew, I'd say, and the man is a 'man of the yew', Fer Í, the name of the little harper we met earlier on in Lady Gregory's story of Aine and the bad judgement of Oilioll over Fer Í that led to the death of himself and his seven sons at the battle of Mucruimhe, or Mucrama, a place near Athenry, County Galway, homeland of Michael Furey. 'Furey' is a variant, I suggest, of Fer Í. That 'Í' is itself a truncated version of *ibar* or *iobhar* or *iubhar*, the yew tree whose red wood is famous for, among other things, lining the walls of the Red Branch palace at Emain Macha (the 'neck-bodkin' of

Macha) and the making of breastplates. And, wouldn't you know it, *iobhar* is a near version of 'Ivors', that breastplated, neck-bodkined young woman who sets her *Western Gael*-oshes in contention against Gabriel's West Briton *Gall*-oshes. Miss Ivors's calling Gabriel a 'West Briton' evokes a tradition of rhetoric including Yeats ('the shoddy society of "West Britonism" ') and Hyde, who writes, again in 'The Necessity For De-Anglicizing Ireland':

I have no hesitation at all in saying that every Irish-feeling Irishman, who hates the reproach of West-Britonism, should set himself to encourage the efforts which are being made to keep alive our once great national tongue.[44]

Miss Ivors, the embodiment of that 'reproach of West-Britonism', is also the embodiment of Ireland itself, since her name might also be construed as a play on Iverne, one Latinized form of the name of the country also known as Hibernia. She certainly stands for something beyond herself, as is evident from Joyce's very deliberate description of her through Gabriel:

Of course the girl or woman, *or whatever she was*, was an enthusiast but there was a time for all things.[45]

The name Ir, as mentioned by Lady Gregory, or Heberus, as mentioned by our friend Giraldus Cambrensis, is cognate with Iberia, if you remember, making the idea of the Milesians being led by a *Mil Espain* less wacky than might first appear. What is 'general' over Ireland is not only the essence of winter, connected as Ireland and winter are in that word 'Hibernia', but what we might call the *Hyper*nian sense of Ireland of which Miss Ivors is the showing forth. Miss *Ivors* may be also a manifestation of *Aoibh*ell, the lover of Dubhlaing ua Artigan, linking her to Bartell D'Arcy and Michael Furey, the *sing*ers at the the centre of the story. That shadowy figure of John Millington *Synge* is only one of several crypto-currents based on names in 'The Dead', names with a specific resonance in the extended field of Celtic studies. The first is notable for not being named, and my sense of his presence is underlined, as with Lady Gregory, by Joyce's resistance, despite his positioning of Gretta at windows with obscured views, to the word 'curtain'. He resists, in

other words, naming Jeremiah Curtin (1838–1906), the folklorist who
had died only the year before the story was written and whose *Myths
and Folklore of Ireland*, published in 1890, includes a story on 'The
Birth of Fin MacCumhail', with the famous incident of Fin's roasting
the salmon of knowledge, burning his thumb, and sucking it by mis-
take. Then there's the story of 'Black, Brown, and Gray', in which Fin
MacCumhail hires the three men of the title to keep watch. Black is
led by a light to a house in which men are drinking from a single cup.
Brown is next led by a light to a house in which men are using a magical knife that cuts meat from a bare bone. Gray is led by a light to a
house full of dead bodies and a hag who feeds on them. Gray kills the
hag but three giants spring up in her place, two of which he and his
dog, Bran, kill. Twenty-one years later a Fear Ruadh, a red-haired
man, comes to Fin and the Fianna, and is taken on for no wage other
than that he be buried on Inis Caol. When that time comes the
Fenians are reluctant to bury him, but Fin sets his body in a coffin on
an old white horse and points him off towards the burying place, followed by himself and twelve Fenians. When the men get there to the
temple on Inis Caol the white horse and the coffin have gone. The
men are fastened to their seats and can't get up:

At that moment the Fear Ruadh stood before them in all his former strength
and youth and said: 'Now is the time for me to take satisfaction out of you for
my mother and brothers.' Then one of the men said to Fin, 'Chew your
thumb to know is there any way out of this.'[46]

This strategem of thumb-chewing saves Fin yet again. It's a throw-
back to the salmon-roasting episode and it clarifies, yet again, a
moment that is otherwise somewhat banal. That's the story told by
Mrs Malins about her son-in-law in Scotland. 'One day he caught a
fish, a beautiful big big fish, and the man in the hotel boiled it for their
dinner.' The image of the white horse in the story of 'Black, Brown,
and Gray' also helps make sense of another throwaway line from Miss
O'Callaghan on the ride back to the Gresham:

They say you never cross O'Connell Bridge without seeing a white horse.
I see a white man this time, said Gabriel.

That 'white man' may be a version of Fionn, 'the white one', which would be appropriate of the hero, Daniel O'Connell, who occupies the liminal/narthecal position Douglas Hyde afforded him in 'The Necessity for De-Anglicizing Ireland'. The fact that the line about the 'white horse' is given to Miss O'Callaghan is significant also, since *cailleach* means a 'veiled woman, a nun, a woman celibate, an old woman, a hag', connecting her to the hag in the story, a story about a feast in which there is a general paralysis among the guests, of whom there seem to be thirteen, as well as the ghostly Fear Ruadh, another near version of Furey, who's associated with *'Nun's* Island'. (We might remember that, according to Lady Gregory, Ir, with whom Furey is linked through his 'western' associations with Miss Ivors, was buried on the monastic island of Sceilg *Michill.*) The song Michael Furey sings, 'The Lass of Aughrim', is a version of Ballad 76 in the great collection of Francis James Child, with whom Jeremiah Curtin had studied folklore at Harvard. A second ghostly presence here is Alfred Nutt (1856–1910) who appears as the *'nutmeg'* on the table at the banquet. His *Studies on the Legend of the Holy Grail*, published in 1888, emphasized the Irish element in the Arthurian legends. I'm not going to try here to crack Nutt, or Arthurian motifs in 'The Dead', except perhaps to mention the standing army of Fenian bottles, 'black, with brown and red labels', dedicated to Arthur Guinness, because I know you already think I'm totally nuts. Let me suggest, instead, that another guest at the Morkans' party, Bergin, is more likely than not to be Osborn Bergin (1873–1950). So far as I can make out, Bergin would have been teaching at the School of Irish Learning in Dublin in 1904, and he would already have been at work on his great edition of *Stories from Keating's History of Ireland*, published in 1909, which includes accounts of the death of Connor by the brain-ball, the death of Ceat, and the death of Cú Roí. Cú Roí, whose name might be rendered as Conroy, has a magical fortress which revolves, in the style of Patrick Morkan's horse, on its axis. Cú Roí is betrayed by his wife, Blathnaid, daughter of Connor MacNessa, to her lover, Cuchulainn, who waits outside the fort for a signal from her. The signal is the whitening of a stream when Blathnaid pours a churn of milk into it. This whitening is replayed, I think, in the 'general' whitening of Ireland, which Gabriel Conroy takes to be a direct signal for action, so that 'the time had come for him to start out on his journey westward'. We've seen how Joyce's conglomewriting allows him to conflate and transfer aspects of one character to another, so that Gabriel includes aspects of both the 'betrayed' Cú Roí and the battle-ready Cuchulainn, ready to fight with the 'shades'. For once, Cuchulainn shares his chariot with his enemy, Ferdia, who appears here as *Freddy* Malins. Freddy has characteristics commonly associated with Cuchulainn, of course, particularly his *riastarthae*, or 'convulsions', generally translated as his 'warp-spasm', in which his features and limbs are violently dislocated. You might remember how Freddy is described twice within two pages as 'rubbing the knuckles of his left fist backwards and forwards into his left eye'. In the same paragraph we find, 'Freddy Malins *exploded*'.[47] The relationship between Cuchulainn and Cu Roi is central to the narrative of *Fled Bricrenn: The Feast of Bricriu*, with which Joyce is likely to have been familiar from the 1899 edition translated by George Henderson. At its centre is a party and the idea of the allocation of the *curadmír*, or 'champion's portion' of pork, which leads to long-running competition between Loegaire Buadach, Conall Carnach, Cuchulainn, and Cú Roí, towards the end of which Cú Roí appears as a giant headless churl who concedes defeat to Cuchulainn, and gives him the champion's portion in perpetuity, because of Cuchulainn's bravery in offering him his neck for beheading. The allotting of the 'champion's portion' appears in 'The Dead' as the 'invidious task' faced by Gabriel Conroy of choosing between the 'Three Graces'. (If Kate is Ket or MacCecht, by the way, as I take to be substantiated by a detail offered by Joyce appropriate to a 'champion's portion'—Aunt Kate . . . had been *picking a bone*'[48]—I take Julia to be a version of Oilioll, with whom the idea of both music and 'judgement' are associated, while the 'Three Graces' are reminiscent of those three generous sons of Lugaidh Men, from that other Lady Gregory story of *Gods and Fighting Men*.) In any event, Gabriel refers in his speech to the assembled crowd, for whom he has carved the goose, as their having been 'the recipients—or perhaps, I had better say, the *victims*—of the hospitality of certain good ladies'.[49] Gabriel's been worried earlier in the evening about this speech, fearing that at least one reference in it would be '*above the heads* of his hearers'.[50] The reference is to 'the lines from Robert Browning', which he plans to use in his speech, and by the way, I'm going to go out on a limb here to suggest that the quotation from Browning that would have gone, literally, 'over the heads' of his audience is from 'Paracelsus'. This is a poem in which we find not only the phrase 'I go to prove my soul', an idea picked up by Joyce for the second-to-last sentence of *A Portrait of the Artist as a Young Man* ('*I* go to encounter for the millionth time the reality of experience and to forge in the smithy of my *soul* the uncreated conscience of my race') but this:

Measure your mind's height by the shade it casts.[51]

This would be the perfect quotation for a speech focusing on judgement, as well as an embodiment of the 'gnomon'. Even if he doesn't allude to Browning in his speech, the poet is much on Gabriel's mind, if only because of Miss Ivors's cutting remarks about his 'review of Browning's poems'. Quite which these poems are is unclear, since Browning's *Poetical Works* had long-since been published, however one dates the Morkans' party, in 1888–9. My hunch is that G.C. is reviewing the publication, in 1903, of G. K. Chesterton's *Robert Browning*, in which Chesterton wrote:

His mysticism was not of that idle and wordy type which believes that a flower is symbolical of life; it was rather of that deep and eternal type which believes that life, a mere abstraction, is symbolical of the flower.[52]

I suspect that something of this is carried over by Gabriel to his musing on Gretta's standing in the shadow at the top of the stairs, 'He asked himself what is a woman standing on the stairs in the shadow, listening to distant music, a symbol of.' Chesterton is responding here, in part, to George Santayana's dissatisfaction, as voiced in 'The Poetry of Barbarism', with Browning's methods which, as he describes them, sound remarkably like some of Joyce's:

Even his short poems have no completeness, no limpidity. They are little torsos made broken so as to stimulate the reader to the restoration of their missing arms and legs. What is admirable in them is pregnancy of phrase, vividness of passion and sentiment, occasional beauties of versification,—all like

the quick sharp scratch
And blue spurt of a lighted match.[53]

This last phrase comes from 'Meeting at Night', and is preceded immediately by 'A tap at the pane',[54] which is precisely the image Joyce uses to instigate the last paragraph of the story:

A few light *taps upon the pane* made him turn to the window. It had begun to snow again. He watched sleepily the flakes, silver and dark, falling obliquely against the lamplight. The time had come for him to set out on his journey westward.

We've seen Joyce use the free-associative mimeticism we associate with Browning to point up an allusion, as in his description of Miss Ivors, as 'the girl or woman, or whatever she was', or to 'Erinize' a situation, as in Gabriel's monodramatic description of his own 'riot of emotions'. These last passages of 'The Dead' are deliberately overwritten, drawing on a tired use of inversion—'He watched sleepily'—and inverted repetition—'falling softly' followed by 'softly falling', 'falling faintly' followed by 'faintly falling'—to underscore what Gabriel, and Joyce, recognize as the worn, if welcoming, rhetoric of the late nineteenth-century proponents of cultural nationalism. This 'Erinizing' I speak of is prepared by Joyce's allowing Gabriel to comment on his asking 'ironically' of Gretta if Michael Furey was 'Someone you were in love with?' A little later this exchange takes place:

What was he? asked Gabriel, still ironically.
He was in the gasworks, she said.
Gabriel felt humiliated by *the failure of his irony* and by the evocation of this figure from the dead, a boy in the gasworks.[55]

This 'Eriny', which we shouldn't fail to miss on this occasion, is yet another device used by Joyce to ensure that 'The Dead' is indeed a story of 'public life', in which Joyce undercuts the rhetoric of cultural nationalism, revelling in the very thing he repudiates, delighting in what he disdains. It's a brilliantly effective way of addressing an issue raised by Gabriel, confronted by Miss Ivors, when 'he wanted to say that literature was above politics'. Joyce knows that literature is never above politics, that they coexist in a form of what we might call 'Irwiny', in which Thomas Caulfield Irwin's 'umbrella and a revolver' are in a stand-off against John O'Donovan's 'houseful of books'.

# Kavanagh

The stand-off, or 'temporary wrangle' has rarely been so brilliantly presented, at least in the lyric poem, as in 'Epic' by Patrick Kavanagh (1905–67). Here Kavanagh gives us an image of two neighbouring families, the Duffys and McCabes, who are in dispute over a boundary:

> I heard the Duffys shouting 'Damn your soul'
> And old McCabe stripped to the waist, seen
> Step the plot defying blue cast-steel—
> 'Here is the march along these iron stones'.
> That was the year of the Munich bother. Which
> Was the more important? I inclined
> To lose my faith in Ballyrush and Gortin
> Till Homer's ghost came whispering to my mind.
> He said: I made the Iliad from such
> A local row. Gods make their own importance.[56]

The dispute is one John O'Donovan would recognize as having to do with a field- or parish-boundary, but the 'iron' in 'these iron stones' is a near version of 'Erin', so we're dealing with a national dispute as well. Then there's the international aspect of 'That was the year of the Munich bother'. Kavanagh wrote this poem in 1951, a year after John Hewitt's 'The Colony', and I'm tempted to think Kavanagh was aware of the Hewitt poem. Kavanagh's poem was first published in *The Bell* in November 1951, along with 'On Looking into E. V. Rieu's Homer' which includes the lines:

> The intensity that radiated from
> The Far Field Rock—you afterwards denied—
> Was the half-god seeing his half-brothers
> Joking on the fabulous mountainside.[57]

This seems to come in a direct line from AE's little poem 'Exiles', though it also borrows from the 'mythic method' of Joyce, as is evidenced by the fact that Kavanagh's next published poem, in the April 1951 number of *Envoy*, is 'Who Killed James Joyce?'. This is a light-hearted satire in the spirit of his 1949 poem *The Paddiad*:

> In the corner of a Dublin pub
> This party opens—blub-a-blub—
> Paddy Whiskey, Rum and Gin
> Paddy Three Sheets in the Wind;
> Paddy of the Celtic mist,
> Paddy Connemara West,
> Chestertonian Paddy Frog
> Croaking nightly in the bog.
> All the paddies having fun
> Since Yeats handed in his gun.[58]

This hellish 'Hellenization' of Ireland appeals not only to Joyce, but to Yeats himself, who in his introduction to *Gods and Fighting Men*, wrote:

Was it not Aeschylus who said he but served up dishes from the banquet of Homer? But Homer himself found the great banquet on an earthen floor and under a broken roof. We do not know who at the foundation of the world made the banquet for the first time . . . but we do know that, unless those that have made many inventions are about to change the nature of poetry, we may have to go where Homer went if we are to sing a new song.[59]

Yeats's sense of the possibility of following Homer was influenced in turn by the rhetoric of O'Grady, who wrote, in the paragraph immediately following that about 'the dim twilight region, where day meets night', that the legends of a country

present a rhythmic completeness and a beauty not to be found in the fragmentary and ragged succession of events in time. Achilles and Troy appear somehow more real than Histiaeus and Miletus, Cuchulain and Emain Macha than Brian Boru and Kincora.[60]

What Kavanagh has learned from Yeats and Joyce, as they learned from O'Grady, Hyde, and Ferguson, is an almost total reliance upon the 'earthern floor' and the 'broken roof'. He does exhibit a slight failure of nerve, even in this great poem, by overly insisting on his theme. The fact that he uses the word 'important' in the first line of the poem, 'I have lived in important places', takes away from the impact of the last line. 'Gods make their own importances' is an allusion, of course, to Browning's title *Dis Aliter Visum*, itself a quotation from Book II of the *Aeneid*, though that allusion is almost entirely hidden. I'll be looking in even more detail at this arcane and esoteric aspect of several other Irish writers, including C. S. Lewis, Thomas MacGreevy, and Louis MacNeice, in my next chapter.

# 3

## 'Alone Tra La'

# Le Fanu

I'D like to concentrate on that aspect of Irish writing, as embodied in the gnomic utterances of the first Irish poet, Amergin, that has to do with what Robert Graves described as the 'esoteric' or 'pied', what I described previously as 'the urge towards the cryptic, the encoded, the runic, the virtually unintelligible'. The word 'runic' itself derives from the Old English word *run*, akin to the Old Norse *run* and, believe it or not, the Old Irish *rún*—all combining ideas of a 'secret' or a 'secret conversation' and, as defined by the *OED*, 'a letter or character or mark . . . having mysterious or magical powers attributed to it', 'an incantation or charm', or 'any song, poem or verse'. I'll concentrate here on the runic as it exhibits itself in the love poem, and the genre of political love poem known as the *aisling*, a word generally translated as 'dream vision', but which might be more accurately termed a 'vision-voyage'. This delight in the idea of the 'vision-voyage' coincides with a delight in ventriloquism, or voice throwing, that allows the individual to make manifest a multiplicity of points of view, including political points of view, allowing him or her the freedom to shape-shift with all the aplomb exhibited by Amergin himself, in what I again described previously as 'his tireless reinvention of himself as stag or flood or wind or tear or hawk'.

That idea of 'tireless reinvention of himself' is one that would have found favour with Joseph Sheridan Le Fanu (1814–73), the son of a Church of Ireland rector based just outside Dublin, whose reputation as a leading 'sensationalist' and associate member of the great triumvirate of Irish Gothic writers that includes Maturin, Stoker, and himself seems better founded and grounded than several of his plots. Le Fanu's extraordinarily complex novel *The House by the Church-Yard*[1] seems to be at least partly autobiographical. Set in 1767 in what was then the village of Chapelizod, near what will become Phoenix Park, and where his father had his living, it's a story told by a certain Charles Cresseron about Sturk, the shoemaker who recognizes the character Paul Dangerfield to be in fact Charles Archer, recognizes him from twenty years earlier to be the murderer of Kilwarden, a murder for which an innocent man, Lord Dunoran, has already been found guilty. With me so far? Sturk is the victim of a violent attack by an unknown assailant which leaves him comatose. After a brain-operation, Sturk comes to his senses for long enough to point the finger at Dangerfield/Archer. We recognize some of these elements, perhaps, from *Finnegans Wake*, at the heart of which is a crime having to do with what Joyce refers to, in his garbling of St Augustine's *O felix culpa*, as 'O foenix culprit'.[2] The crime that takes place in Phoenix Park is, as you know, already an amalgam of some indiscretion involving Humphrey Chimpden Earwicker, three fusiliers and three young women, and the murders of Cavendish and Burke by the Invincibles so memorably rendered by Sir Samuel Ferguson in 'At the Polo Ground'. This tendency towards the amalgam, the tendency for one event or character to blur and bleed into another, what I've called elsewhere an 'imarrhage', is a staple of *Finnegans Wake*. In many cases, there is no delineation, indeed, between person and place. This association of person and place is at least as old as the anonymous sixth-century poem in which 'the flank of Tailtiu' is one with 'the flank of Aed Mac Ainmirech'. In the case of *Finnegans Wake*, Chapelizod bleeds into Isolde, after whom it is named. Isolde bleeds into young Eve, Eve into the Esthers—Johnson and Vanhomrigh (Swift's 'Stella' and 'Vanessa')—the Esthers into Alice, 'Alas in jumboland'[3] into Isabel, the fictional Isabel into Joyce's real-life daughter, Lucia. That Lucia should herself suffer from a form of schizophrenia known as hebephrenia which, according to Richard Ellmann, is 'characterized by hallucinations, absurd delusions, silly mannerisms, and other kinds of deterioration'[4] is surely significant, though no less so than Ellmann's brilliantly casual comment that 'Joyce had a remarkable capacity to follow her swift jumps of thought which baffled other people completely.'[5]

# Lewis

Let me swiftly jump ahead here to consider for a moment an aspect of the many-aspected C. S. Lewis (1898–1963) which connects him to

James Joyce in what is, for me at least, an unexpected way. Among C. S. Lewis's lesser-known distinctions, one of which I just happened to read in the *1998 Irish Almanac and Yearbook of Facts*, was the 'fact' that he was the 'father of actor Daniel Day Lewis'. This is ample evidence in itself for our tendency to confuse and conflate, understandable perhaps in the case of an actor of such protean talents and a writer whose gift manifested itself in such a wide range of ways, from his great study of courtly love, *The Allegory of Love*, through his beautifully clear and direct *Mere Christianity*, to his sci-fi trilogy that includes *That Hideous Strength*, in which the figure of Merlin is supposedly based partly on W. B. Yeats. I'll concentrate here, though, on one or two key aspects of *The Chronicles of Narnia*, Lewis's best-known work. This is a series of seven tales, the first of which, *The Lion, the Witch and the Wardrobe*, was published in 1950. You'll remember the basic premiss. Four children are 'sent away from London during the war because of the air-raids' to a house belonging to an old Professor, presumably something of a self-portrait by Lewis. One of the children, Lucy, is drawn by an unexplained noise towards a wardrobe:

Looking into the inside, she saw several coats hanging up—mostly long fur coats. There was nothing Lucy liked so much as the smell and feel of fur . . . Soon she went further in and found that there was a second row of coats hanging up behind the first one.[6]

I want to suggest that here we have a combination of what is by now an all-too-familiar narthex, the antechamber to some contiguous realm, and the conventional *féth fiada* of which I've made so much. It has the conventional prelude of an inexplicable noise, the *ceol sídhe*, or fairy music. The *féth fiada* also usually has the appearance of a wild animal, a deer, and this case is no exception:

He was only a little taller than Lucy herself and he carried over his head an umbrella, white with snow . . . He was a Faun.[7]

The Faun is the animal conventionally associated with the *féth fiada* for a good, very simple reason, I suspect. It has to do with the pun on the words *fiadh*, a 'deer', and *fiadha*, a 'lord', the 'lord' being a person who was allowed to engage in the activity of *fiadhach*, or 'hunting'.

The association between the deer and the lord are evident in the names of the son and grandson of Fionn, the 'white' one, whose name is, I think, cognate with 'fawn', though most linguists would probably disagree with that, insisting that it comes directly from *faunus*. The 'Fi' element in Fionn is related, I suspect, to that '*fi*' in *fiadh*. The name Oisin certainly means 'fawn'. The name Oscar certainly means 'beloved of the deer'. The signal to Oisin of a contiguous Land of Youth is an *eilit maol*, or 'hornless doe'. The liminality of the Faun in *The Lion, the Witch and the Wardrobe* is compounded by his name, Mr Tumnus. I take 'Tumnus' to be a near version of *terminus*, a 'boundary', with an echo of *tumulus*, the 'mound' associated with the *féth fiadh*, with a ghost of 'Cernunnos', the antlered god, waiting in the wings, not to speak of a hint of *Dominus*, the mediating 'Lord'. The country into which Mr Tumnus welcomes Lucy is, of course, Narnia. What can we say about Narnia? The first thing to be said about it is that 'snow is general' over the country. For the first thing Lucy notices as she walks through the narthecal wardrobe is that

Something cold and soft was falling on her. A moment later she found that she was standing in the middle of a wood at night-time with snow under her feet and snowflakes falling through the air. Lucy felt a little frightened, but she felt very inquisitive and excited as well. She looked back over her shoulder and there, between the dark tree trunks, she could still see the open doorway of the wardrobe and even catch a glimpse of the empty room from which she had set out.[8]

It's not too much to say, I hope, that 'the empty room from which she had set out' is a version of the room in the Gresham Hotel from which Gabriel Conroy 'must *set out* on his journey westward'. The appearance of the Faun, Mr Tumnus, combines elements of the 'tree' we associate with Michael Furey and the 'ghostly light of the street lamp' outside the hotel room:

She began to walk forward, *crunch-crunch,* over the snow and through the wood towards the other light. In about ten minutes she reached it and found that it was a lamp-post. As she stood looking at it, wondering why there was a lamp-post in the middle of a wood and wondering what to do next, she heard the pitter patter of feet coming towards her. And soon after that a very strange person stepped out from among the trees into the light of the lamp-post.[9]

The distant, beckoning light is, as we know, another feature of the conventional *féth fiada*. The Narnia into which Lucy is transported is, we discover, a land in which 'it is winter . . . and has been for ever so long'. This Narnia is, then, in addition to being a near version of 'Erne' or 'Erin', another version of Hibernia, the 'winter/Ireland' that dominates 'The Dead'. The connection between the story and this land in which 'it is winter . . . and has been for ever so long' is brought home in the same sentence when Mr Tumnus announces that 'we shall both catch cold if we stand here talking in the snow'.[10] The fate of Michael Furey ('I implored him to go home at once and told him he would get his death in the rain') is not to befall Mr Tumnus and Lucy or, as she's known familiarly, Lu. This 'Lu' is meant to bring to mind the Celtic god Lugh, who manifests himself is an astonishing array of characters with an astonishing array of skills in an astonishing range of places. His name is thought to be an element of place names as far flung as Lyons, Leiden, and Luguballium, now better known as Carlisle. Lugh is a Celtic version of Mercury and, as such, presents himself variously as a carpenter, a smith, and a harper. He is also a messenger or guide, a role taken on by Lucy when she returns from Narnia with news of the political climate there and leads the other children on a return expedition. This 'climate' is recognizable from a Joycean conglomewriting of several Celtic sources, I think, one or two of them Irish. The first Irish source is *Baile in Scáil*, known in English as 'The Phantom's Frenzy' or 'The Poetic Ecstasy of the Phantom'. The phantom in question is Lugh himself, who appears to Conn of the Hundred Battles with his wife, the goddess Ériu, and serves him great portions of meat at a feast in a splendid palace. When Ériu offers ale to the company, she asks to whom the cup should be given and Lugh gives a list of names of princes, then disappears, palace and all. The figure of Ériu is also known as the Sovranty of Ireland, described by Roger S. Loomis in his entry on the festival of *Lughnasadh* in the 1949 edition of Funk and Wagnalls's *Standard Dictionary of Folklore, Mythology and Legend*:

It seems, then, that Lugh's bride was the Sovranty of Ireland, but a number of stories relate how one or another of the destined kings of Ireland mated with the Sovranty of Ireland, transforming her from a monstrous hag into a radiant beauty . . . For we learn of Ériu that she was of the Tuatha Dé danann, took many shapes, and was the wife of MacGréni, 'son of the Sun'. The metamorphosis of the Sovranty of Ireland, therefore, is a blurred version of a nature myth, in which the future kings of Ireland have inherited the role of Lugh, the sun god, while the hag is the land of Ireland, transformed by the carresses of the sun from the bleakness of winter into the floral splendor of spring—a version of the widespread myth of the union of sun and earth.[11]

A 'blurred version' of this 'blurred version of a nature myth' is at the centre of *The Lion, the Witch and the Wardrobe*. The battle between the forces of winter and summer remains constant, of course, but the 'hag' is transmogrified into the 'White Witch', a force of evil, while Lugh appears partly as Lucy, as we've seen, and partly as the *li*on, Aslan. Lucy's name is also a near version of our guide and multi-faceted artificer, '*Lew*is', who more than likely knew the work of the Celtic scholar *Loo*mis, perhaps even met him when Loomis was a student at Oxford. I think he must have read Loomis in Funk and Wagnalls, at least, partly because of the propinquity of a phrase in the entry on Lugh, above the initials RSL, on the page immediately before the entry on *Lughnasa*:

In the *Prophetic Ecstasy*, Lugh appears as a supernatural horseman, who summoned Conn to his palace and there, though he declared that he was a son of Adam and had returned after death, he foretold the names of the rulers of Tara.[12]

This term, 'son of Adam', and its female equivalent, 'daughter of Eve', is used by Mr Tumnus to describe the humans in Narnia, that country that 'lies between the lamp-post and the great castle of Cair Paravel on the eastern sea'.[13] The name 'Cair Paravel' suggests at once the terminus-marking, Hermetic *cairn*, or pile of stones, and a near version of 'Perceval' or 'Percival'. It is our friend, Roger S. Loomis, who's also responsible for the entries on both Percival and the Grail in Funk and Wagnalls's *Standard Dictionary of Folklore*. In the entry on the Grail, Loomis writes of the connections between *The Poetic Ecstasy of the Phantom* with Éiru asking Lugh to whom the cup should be given and the Grail quest:

Not only is this sequence of events dimly recognizable in Perceval's visit to the Grail castle, not only is the question echoed in the meaningless question test, but also Lug's lightning spear is the prototype of the bleeding lance, and Ireland personified is one of the prototypes of the Grail bearer, for both these stately damsels assume elsewhere a hideous shape.[14]

Loomis expands on the spear and the lance in his entry on Lancelot:

The great Irish sun god Lugh bore the epiphet *lamfada*, 'Long Hand'. Lugh was taken over by the Welsh as Lluch Llauynnauc . . . The accident that *lluch* as a common noun meant 'lake' led to the conversion of the name Lluch into the title 'du Lac' . . . The account . . . of Lancelot's rescue of Guinevere and his four combats with her abductor, Meleagant, who is elsewhere called Melvas, king of the Summer Country, reflects the seasonal myth of the abduction of a flower maiden and the annual combats for her possession between the personifications of summer and winter. . . . Thus Lancelot's legend is the result of successive accretions made by Welsh and Breton reciters and French romancers to the original Irish myths of the divine Lugh.[15]

# Mac Cumhaigh

Not only does the name *Lancelot* find its echo in *Aslan*, but the name of the lion conjures up, is a near version of, the term *aisling* I used earlier on. The *aisling* or 'vision-voyage' is a quite specific genre of eighteenth-century political poem, one of the most famous of which was written by Art Mac Cumhaigh (1738?–73) and is entitled, unsurprisingly, *Aisling Airt Mhic Cumhaigh*:

> Ag cuan Bhinn Éadain ar bhruach na hÉireann,
>    Agus me ar thaobh tonn na bóchna 'mo luí,
> Tháinig aisling bhéalbhinn gan fhios do m'fhéachaint,
>    Ar aiste Vénus no i gcló bean sí:
> Agus duirt gur éirigh as an Chreagan céad fear
>    De mhaithibh Gael as na tuambaibh aníos,
> Is go raibh Síol Néill ina mbeathaibh saora,
>    Is an Feadh ag géilleadh doibh in ór 's i maoin.[16]

This might be rendered into English as:

> As I lay out by Howth Harbor, on the edge of Erin,
>    As I lay out by the oceanside,

A sweet-mouthed vision would take me unawares
    In the guise of some Venus or fairy bride.
She told me that a hundred men of the native-born gentry
    Had risen up from their cold, cold graves
And the O'Neills were once more alive and free
    To collect from the Fews their gold-tribute and tithes.

Several things come to mind here. The location, first of all. *Beann Eadair* or *Beann Eadain* is the 'peak' or 'mount of Etain', whom we know, if only from Sir Samuel Ferguson's 'Aideen's Grave' and Lady Gregory's retelling in *Gods and Fighting Men* of the tale of 'Midhir and Etain'. The first significant aspect of this situation is that it already has associations with a supernatural presence. You recall from Lady Gregory how a spell is cast on this supernatural lover, Etain, in which Angus 'made a sunny house for her, and put sweet smelling flowers in it, and he made invisible walls about it, that no one could see through and that could not be seen'.[17] I'm quite sure Joyce is aware of this passage when he situates so much of the sun- and flower-filled Molly Bloom's soliloquy on Howth Head, the English name for *Beann Eadair* or *Beann Eadain*. For Art Mac Cumhaigh, the siting of his vision on Howth Head is significant in that it points to his dislocation from his native realm, the Fews of South Armagh, some one hundred and fifty miles to the north. *An Feadh* or *na Feadha* means simply 'the woods', from the word *fiodh*, meaning 'a tree, a wood, a letter *esp.* of the ogham alphabet'. From his vantage point on Howth Head, however, Mac Cumhaigh can see the hills of South Armagh, hills now almost certainly cleared of their trees as they are, increasingly, of those who would recognize the connection between a 'tree' and a 'letter of the alphabet' in the word *fiodh*. I'll go out on a limb of the alphabet tree for a moment to suggest that there's a connection between the *fiodh* of the tree, the *fiadh* of the 'deer' among the trees, the *fianna* of the 'deer hunters among the trees', engaged in their *venery*, and the 'Venus' in whose guise the 'sweet-mouthed vision' appears. There's also a strong connection, by the way, between the tales of Fionn and the Fianna and Howth Head, to where they're often drawn by the apparition of a beautiful woman. Joyce alludes to the *aisling* genre on page 179 of *Finnegans Wake*:

It would have diverted, if ever seen, the shuddersome spectacle of this semi-demented zany amid the inspissated grime of his glaucous den making believe to read his usylessly unreadable Blue Book of Eccles, édition de ténèbres . . . telling himself delightedly, no espellor mor so, that every splurge on the vellum he blundered over was an aisling vision more gorgeous than the one before t.i.t.s., a roseschelle cottage by the sea for nothing for ever . . .[18]

The 'Blue Book of Eccles' is, of course, the 'usyless' *Ulysses*, and this appellation is meant to bring to mind a number of Irish manuscript volumes, particularly *The Yellow Book of Lecan*, which included versions of *Táin Bó Cuailnge* and *Togail Bruidne Da Derga*, 'The Destruction of Da Derga's Hostel'. The 'aisling vision more gorgeous than the one before t.i.t.s.' cuts immediately to the sexual aspect of the woman. The word *cuan* in *'cuan Bhinn Éadain'* means a 'bend, a curve, a hollow place, a recess, a harbour' and is cognate with the words *cunneus*, a wedge, and *cone* and *coney*, the rabbit that lives in a wedge- or cone-shaped hole, as well as an indelicate term for the female part. The *binn* in the genetive case in *'cuan Bhinn Eadain'* prepares the way for the *'aisling bhéalbhinn'*, the sweet-mouthed vision in the next line. The pun on *'bhinn'* as 'peak' and *'bhinn'* as 'sweet' allows for a reading of that first line, indeed, as 'In the sweet recess of Etain', while yet another meaning of *beann* is given by the ever-coy Father Dinneen as 'lap'. This sexually charged landscape is further extended by the use of the word *bruach*, a 'brink, edge, bank, border, boundary, shore or coast' that is cognate in Irish with the word *brú*, 'the womb, the belly, the breast, bosom', as it is, I think (unconventionally, I know) with the 'brooch' such as the one on Miss Ivors's bodice. That's why Joyce focuses on the 't.i.t.s.' in that passage from *Finnegans Wake*. This sexualization and personification of the landscape is included in the very place name *Creagan*, a word cognate with the English word 'crag', and meaning 'a little rock, a rocky or stony place, a blank spot in a growing crop, a bruise or sore'. The personification of the land-scape extends, in Mac Cumhaigh's work itself, to the throwing of the voice through inanimate objects, including one dialogue between the poet and Glasdrummond Castle, another between a Protestant church and a Catholic chapel. More usually, of course, the dialogue is between the poet and the 'sweet-mouthed vision', as it is in another of

Art Mac Cumhaigh's *aislingi*, set in the churchyard at Creggan itself, and entitled *Ur-Chill an Chreagain*:

> Ag úr-chill an Chreagain 'sé chodail mé aréir faoi bhrón
> Is le héiri na maidne tháinig ainnir fá mo dhéin le póig;
> Bhi gríos-ghruaidh ghartha aici, agus loinnir ina ciabh mar ór,
> 'S gurbh é íochshláinte an domhain bheith ag amharc ar an ríon óig.[19]

This opening might be rendered as follows:

> In the churchyard at Creggan I slept last night, all forlorn,
> And a maiden came to me with a kiss at morn;
> What with her blush-bright cheek and her hair's golden sheen,
> It did my heart good to gaze at that lovely young queen.

One of the conventions of the *aisling* form is that much is made of the possible identity of the *spéirbhean*, or 'sky-woman', who appears to the poet, who in turn takes the opportunity to show off his grasp of classical mythology, enquiring if she's Helen, or the wife of Orpheus, or one of the nine muses of Parnassus, *na Naoi mBéithe*. Though the possibility of any one of multiple identities seems to be allowed for, it always turns out that the 'sky-woman' is a version of 'Eriu' or the 'Sovranty of Ireland'. The 'sky-woman' mourns the defeats at the Boyne (1690) and Aughrim (1691), that's to say the defeat of James by the Williamites, and other 'bruises' and 'sores' for which there is no *íochshláinte*, or balm, including the demise of the Gaelic language:

> 'Tá mo chroí-se réabtha 'na mhíle céad cuid,
>      Agus balsam féin nach bhfóireann mo phian,
> Nuair a chluinim an Ghalig uilig da tréigbheáil,
>      Agus caismirt Bhéarla i mbeol gach aoin,
> Bhullaigh is Jane ag glacadh léagsai,
>      Ar dhúichibh Éireann na mor-bhall caoin
> 'S nuair a fiafraim scéala 'sé freagra gh'ibhim:
>      "You're a papist, I know not thee." '[20]

> 'My heart is in a hundred thousand bits, all burst and broken,
>      And there's no balm that will give me relief
> When I hear the Irish language everywhere forsaken
>      And a tra la of English in everybody's mouth,
> Willie and Jane are taking out long lets

> On those great tracts of Ireland so steeped in history
> And if ever I inquire about it, there's only one answer I get:
> "You're a Papist, I know not thee." '

The macaronic aspect of *Aisling Airt Mhic Cumhaigh*, its mingling and mangling of language, is picked up by Joyce in that phrase in *Finnegans Wake* I quoted earlier:

no espellor mor so

The 'mor' is a 'more' without an 'e', but in Irish *mór* means 'big' or 'great', so that the sentence is garbled, on the borderline between sense and nonsense. The 'so' could be seen as a truncated version of Seoighe or O'Seoighe, Joyce's name in Irish. (Joyce puns on one version of his name, *An tSeoigheach* ('The Joyce') and *an tseabhach*, 'the hawk', in his description of Stephen Dedalus as 'a hawklike man flying sunward above the sea'.)[21] 'Mor so' could therefore be construed as 'Great Joyce'. The 'no', in addition, means 'or' in Irish. This macaronic garble applies also to the word 'espellor', a word that goes in four or five directions at once. On one hand, it includes the word 'speller', both in the sense of someone with a skill in spelling out words and a dealer in spells or charms, confirming, as in the case of 'rune', the indivisibility of the ideas of writing and secrecy, and their indivisibility from a notion of power. It might be read as a near version of 'gospeller', minus the 'g'. Beyond that, though, it has two meanings of which I'm certain Joyce is aware. There's 'speller' meaning 'a set of antlers', a word suggesting the idea of cuckoldry at the heart of the Blue Book of Eccles, as well as relating to Finn and the deer-chasing Fenians. Then there's the Irish word *speal*, with its genitive case *speile*, meaning a scythe, and cognate, I'd say, with the word 'spelt', meaning a variety of wheat, with which it's symbiotically linked. This is the root of the English word 'spalpeen'. According to the *OED*, this word is 'of uncertain origin and meaning' and we are told that 'the etymology given in the quotation of 1780 is fanciful'. That quotation, from Arthur Young, suggests that 'Connaught labourers . . . are called spalpeens: *spal* in Irish is a scythe and *peen* a penny; that is, a mower for a penny a day'. The quotation is not fanciful, as it happens, and Joyce's association of himself, in the word 'espellor', with these itinerant day-labourers from

the west of Ireland, who worked for almost no return, is at once touching and true.

## MacGreevy

A brief comment on Thomas MacGreevy (1893–1967) and his unlikely
use of the ideas of the *spéirbhean* and the Sovranty of Ireland in one or
two of his poems, beginning with 'Homage to Hieronymus Bosch',
written in 1926:

> A woman with no face walked into the light;
> A boy, in a brown-tree norfolk suit,
> Holding on
> Without hands
> To her seeming skirt.[22]

Like a number of MacGreevy's poems, this is genuinely 'pied' in the
Gravesian sense. That's to say, it's virtually unintelligible without a
supporting apparatus. Who is the 'woman with no face'? Who the
'boy, in a brown-tree norfolk suit'? How can he be 'Holding on | with-
out hands'? Is there some pun on 'seam' in 'her seeming skirt'? We recognize something of this 'skirt', of course, the subtext of a boy
holding on to his mother's skirt, being dependent in an inappropriate
manner. The poem continues with a series of images that are reminiscent of key images in—you've guessed it again—'The Dead'.
We've already had the Gretta-like 'woman with no face' and the
Furey-like 'boy' with his 'tree'. Now it turns out that the woman has
'a group of shadowy figures behind her' on a 'wild wet morning'.
These 'shadowy figures began to stir | When one I had thought dead
| Filmed slowly out of his great effigy on a tomb near by.' This effigy
is reminiscent of the pivotal statue of Daniel O'Connell in 'The
Dead'. The pivotal image of the poem is again familiar:

> High above the Bank of Ireland
> Unearthly music sounded,
> Passing westwards.[23]

These images of the 'unearthly music' and the 'passing westwards'
send the reader back not only to the end of 'The Dead' but the

beginning of the poem, supplementing a faint notion that the woman might be a version of a *speirbhean*, an idea further substantiated by a note in Susan Schreibman's fine edition of the *Collected Poems of Thomas MacGreevy* in which she quotes a recording made by MacGreevy for Harvard University Library:

In Ireland we tend as a result of a poem written by Thomas Davis about 1840 to regard the west of Ireland as the spirit of the nation. When the west is awake, that spirit is awake. When the west is asleep, that spirit is asleep.[24]

These lines on the 'unearthly music' are also commented upon rather memorably by Wallace Stevens in a letter to MacGreevy:

I thought about these lines of yours. Arranged as they are with the reality in the first line one's attention is focused on the reality. Had the order been reversed and had the lines read:

> Unearthly music sounded,
> Passing westwards
> High above the bank of Ireland

the attention would have been focused on what was unreal. You pass in and out of things in your poems just as quickly as the meaning changes in the illustration that I have just used.[25]

Stevens's observation on MacGreevy's ability to 'pass in and out of things' is a perfect description of his method in a poem like *Cron Trath na nDéithe*, or 'The Twilight of the Gods', written in 1923. Set in a cab rattling through the streets of Dublin (a device we recognize now from Joyce out of Ferguson), the poem presents us with a 'heap of broken images' in the manner of Eliot out of Joyce:

> *Folge mir Frau*
> Come up to Valhalla
> To *gile na gile*
> The brightness of brightness
> Towering in the sky
> Over Dublin.[26]

The phrase *Folge mir Frau* means 'Follow me, wife' and comes, I learn from Susan Schreibman, from Wagner's *Das Rheingold*, in which Wotan invites his wife, Fricka, to come with him to Valhalla. The

phrase 'gile na gile' means 'brightness of brightness', and is the title of
an *aisling* by Aodhagan O Rathaille (1670–1728) to which I'll return a
little later. I'll concentrate just now on that notion of the 'brightness
of brightness | *Towering in the sky*'. This is another version of the
'great effigy on the tomb nearby' and, as I mentioned earlier, the
statue of O'Connell in 'The Dead'. It's connected, too, to that other
monument in 'The Dead'—the Wellington Monument. Let's remind
ourselves of Joyce's description of that great pillar:

Meeting a row of upturned faces he raised his eyes to the chandelier
. . . The piano was playing a waltz tune and he could hear the skirts sweeping
against the drawing room door. People, perhaps, were standing in the snow
on the quay outside, gazing up at the lighted windows and listening to the
waltz music. The air was pure there. In the distance lay the park where the
trees were weighted with snow. The Wellington Monument wore a gleaming
cap of snow that flashed westward over the white field of Fifteen Acres.[27]

Let's look at this in detail. The 'upturned faces' are at some remove
from their headhunted bodies, of course, another allusion to the
underpinning of 'The Destruction of Da Derga's Hostel'. We recognize the Wellington Monument as a sly version of the 'galoshes', as in
Wellington *boots*, that are emblematic of West Britonism. We recognize it as an instance of a gnomic *gnomon*, of course, but to what does
it point? I suggest first of all that it points to something beyond itself.
The passage gives several clues to its wish not to be read literally. The
first is the phrase 'People, *perhaps*', with its implication that these people, imagined as they are by Gabriel Conroy, may *not* be people at all.
The second clue is the phrase 'the trees were *weighted* with snow',
which suggests already that this snow, of which we will hear so much
later, is burdened with symbolism. That 'weighted' is a near version of
'freighted' and suggests that the trees might be loaded with ballast.
The faint seagoing aspect of this phrase is amplified by the fact that
the 'people, perhaps' are 'standing . . . on the *quay*' while the noise of
the 'skirts sweeping against the drawing room door', which ushers in
Gabriel's transport, is surely the noise of waves. All of this points to
the idea that this is a version of an *immram* or *imram*, the genre of
'voyage tale' of which the best known are *Imram Brain*, 'The Voyage of
Bran' and one that has a particular resonance for myself, for all too

obvious reasons. That's *Imram Curaig Maile Duin*, 'The Voyage of Muldoon's Curragh'. Now, we know from, among other sources, Maria Tymoczko's *The Irish Ulysses*, that Joyce was familiar with *Imram Curaig Maile Duin* from his namesake P. W. Joyce's *Old Celtic Romances* (1894) and with *Imram Brain* from Kuno Meyer's (1895–7) edition of the tale, with accompanying notes by our old friend, Alfred Nutt. The full title of Meyer's two-volume edition is *The Voyage of Bran Son of Febal to the Land of the Living*, which immediately raises the question of where the 'land of the living' might be situated in relation to the 'land of *the dead*'. *The Voyage of Bran* is also sometimes known as *The Voyage of Bran to the Land of Women*, which is picked up by Joyce in that image of the 'sweeping skirts' in this house dominated by women. The name Bran means 'raven', and we meet him in 'The Dead' as the shape-shifting *Browne* who, if you recall, exhorts the cabman to 'make like a bird for Trinity College'. He would be making like a bird for Trinity College, by the way, because it was there that the manuscript of *Lebor Laignech*, 'The Book of Leinster', in which one version of *The Voyage of Bran* is included, is held. He would be heading 'home'. Again, this makes sense of an otherwise nonsensical moment in 'The Dead'. *Imran Brain* is a seventh- or eighth-century text that exists in a text written down in the eleventh century at the monastery of Druim Sneachta. I was only moderately taken aback to discover recently that a version of 'The Destruction of Da Derga's Hostel' was included in a manuscript compiled there and known as *Cin Dromma Snecht*. There are no prizes for guessing what Druim Sneachta means in Irish. It means 'the ridge of *snow*' and it's one of the reasons why 'people, perhaps, were standing in the snow on the quay outside'. Another reason has to do with that other voyage tale, *Imram Curaig Maíle Dúin*, which was also probably composed in the eighth century and written down in the tenth. It's included in *The Yellow Book of Leccan* I mentioned earlier and, like *Imram Brain*, is a story of a voyage 'westward' undertaken by a young man bent on avenging his father's murder by some pirates. This connects it in Joyce's mind, I believe, to 'The Destruction of Da Derga's Hostel', with the raiders who are attacking the hostel on the Dodder, as does the idea of the violation of a druid's *geis*, or taboo, having to do with the number of people

Muldoon brings with him in the boat. There are three extra, just as there are, in some way, three 'extra' people in the cab that brings Gabriel Conroy to the Gresham Hotel—Bartell d'Arcy, Miss O'Callaghan, and his 'distant' wife. As they gallop along in the actual cab Gabriel has another moment of transport in which he imagines another journey in which he is somehow distanced from himself so that 'Gabriel was again in a cab with her, galloping *to catch the boat*, galloping to their honeymoon'.[28] The 'boat' they're going to 'catch', if we're quick enough to 'catch' it ourselves, is Muldoon's currach. The many strange sights encountered by Muldoon and his men include an island with a beast which 'kept turning himself round and round in his skin . . . like the movement of a flat-lying millstone', a version of Patrick Morkan's horse in the mill, while on another island they meet the Miller of Hell. On yet another, there's a 'crystal bridge', which appears in 'The Dead' as that 'chandelier' to which Gabriel 'raised his eyes'. In another instance, Muldoon and his men are on a 'sea like green crystal', which is carried into 'The Dead' as the double-glassiness of the scene in which Gabriel has a moment of self-recognition:

As he passed in the way of the cheval-glass he caught sight of himself in full length, his broad, well-filled shirt-front, the face whose expression always puzzled him when he saw it in a mirror and his glimmering gilt-rimmed eye-glasses.[29]

This play on 'gilt' and 'guilt', with its echo of the similar play in *Macbeth*, is absolutely consistent with the theme of murder and revenge at the heart of *Imram Curaig Maíle Dúin*. More importantly, there's a crypto-current in the description of Gabriel's 'broad, well-filled shirt-front' which has to do with likening Gabriel to a ship under sail, not inappropriate for a man whose father was 'T. J. Conroy *of the Port and Docks*'.[30] Gabriel has already been 'seen *piloting* Freddy Malins across the landing'[31] in a house in which a dominant feature is a '*pier-glass*'.[32] He's just come from Usher's *Island*, of course, on which Gabriel/Muldoon has met a seductress with 'snow-white skin' and 'a white mantle over her shoulders, which was fastened in front by a silver brooch studded with gold', the famous Miss Ivors with her famous brooch. On another island, Muldoon and his men meet 'smiths . . . striking a large glowing mass of iron . . . sparkling and glowing from the furnace' which Joyce picks up in one of those moments of Gabriel and Gretta's 'secret life together' in that extraordinary image of 'looking in through a grated window at a man making bottles in a furnace'. The 'grated' aspect of that window connects it to the island with 'a silver net hung from the top down to the very water'. This island consists of 'an immense silver pillar standing in the sea. It had eight sides . . . without any land or earth about it, nothing but the boundless ocean, and they could not see its base deep down in the water, neither were they able to see the top on account of its vast height'. Elsewhere, 'the island they saw after this was named Encos, and it was so called because it was supported by a single pillar in the middle'.[33] The 'immense silver pillar' and the island of Encos, which means 'one foot', or 'one leg', are the models for the one-legged Wellington Monument with its 'cap of snow that flashed westward', all its sense of possibility of some 'otherworld' thwarted by the prophylactic 'cap' of snow. This is the background, I suggest, to that image of 'The brightness of brightness | Towering in the sky | Over Dublin' in MacGreevy's *Crón Tráth na nDéithe*.

## MacNeice

As it turns out, *Imram Curaig Maíle Dúin* is also a source-text for Louis MacNeice (1907–63), who drew on it for his 1962 radio play *The Mad Islands*. As MacNeice makes clear in his introduction to the published version of the play, there is a particular attraction for him to the medium of radio that allows for the play's 'jumping about, whether in time or place and between the actual and the fantasy'.[34] MacNeice's Muldoon, by the way, was played in the original Radio Three production by the wonderful Denys Hawthorne, who just happens to be in the audience this afternoon. Muldoon is described in the list of characters as 'a man with a quest'. His journey takes him through a number of the islands with a number of characters I've mentioned, including the Miller of Hell, though they tend to feature anachronistic elements such as uranium, champagne, motor boats, and duffle coats. On several islands, however, we meet characters interpolated by MacNeice, one of whom is up for auction as lot 100, and is described here by another interpolated character called Funster:

Lot 100, ladies and gentlemen, is dying at this moment in the centre of Ireland. She is of advanced years but has been well preserved in hatred. She has not one grey hair on her head nor, even on her deathbed, one tear in her eye . . . One of the great ladies of our day—her name, I'm afraid, is a secret . . . She has plenty of venom in her yet—prolong her life and add a chapter to the annals of Ireland. Any offers for this life which is ebbing away every second. The reserve price is the life of the bidder.[35]

This woman is, of course, Ireland herself, the Sovranty of Ireland. The word 'ebbing' connects her immediately to a 1956 translation by Gerard Murphy of the ninth-century poem about the *Cailleach Bhéirre*, or 'The Old Woman of Beare', a figure sometimes identified as Bui, wife of Lugh Lamfhada:

> Céinmair insi mora máir,
> Dosn-ic tuile íarna traig;
> Os mé, ni frescu dom-í
> Tuile tar éisi n-aithbi.

It is well for an island of the great sea: flood comes to it after its ebb; as for me, I expect no flood after ebb to come to me.[36]

In her Scottish manifestation, this figure is known as *Cailleach Bheur*, and is a daughter of the sun, born old and ugly at the start of winter and renewing herself in spring as a beautiful young woman, just as in *The Lion, the Witch and the Wardrobe*. It's from C. S. Lewis, by the way, that we have one of the earliest snapshots of MacNeice at Oxford. Lewis writes of visiting his student, John Betjeman, in St Aldates on 24 January 1927:

I found myself pitchforked into a galaxy of super-undergraduates, including . . . an absolutely silent and astonishingly ugly person called McNiece, of whom Betjeman said afterwards, 'He doesn't say much, but he's a great poet.'[37]

Lewis's spelling of MacNeice as 'McNiece' is a little better than 'MacPiece', which is how his name appears in *The Cherwell* over the first poem he published while at Oxford. Those variations seem particularly appropriate to a poet who will go on to present himself in so many guises and disguises. It's clear from Jon Stallworthy's biography of *Louis MacNeice* that MacNeice's self-dramatization began at an extraordinarily early age. Stallworthy reproduces a letter written in 1911, when MacNeice was 4, in which he writes of 'going to run away on a raft . . . we will have to go into the interior of North America . . . where the lions howl in the night-time . . . I will disguise myself in an Indian suit and then they will be friends with us.'[38] In a letter to Anthony Blunt, written on 29 March 1927, and quoted by Jon Stallworthy in a note, MacNeice gives a hilarious pedigree for himself that runs on one side from Concobhar MacNessa through St Brandan and Stephen Dedalus to Don Quixote and, on the other, Hamlet through the Playboy of the Western World through Bishop Heber to Queen Victoria.[39] This pedigree is wonderfully revealing, I think. We recognize Concobhar MacNessa, victim of the brain-ball, as the Ulster king with whom MacNeice would want to be identified, though he must also recognize, as MacNeice does, his allegiance as an Ulster Protestant, educated in England, to Queen Victoria. Bishop Heber seems a shade unlikely as a progenitor, until one remembers MacNeice's background as the son of a Church of Ireland bishop who was no doubt familiar with Bishop Heber's hymns. As for Stephen Dedalus, though Lewis doesn't mention it, it's more likely than not that MacNeice was flourishing an ashplant, à la Dedalus, at that party in Betjeman's rooms, such was his identification with him and his creator. In or around the same time as he constructed his pedigree, it seems from Jon Stallworthy, MacNeice delivered a paper on Joyce to the Bodley Society at Merton. The St Brandan listed here by MacNeice is better known, perhaps, as the sixth-century St Brendan of Clonfert, himself the best known of the *seventeen* Irish saints bearing the name. Brendan of Clonfert is the subject of *Navigatio Sancti Brendani Abbatis*, a late ninth- or early tenth-century account of a voyage undertaken by him and fourteen sailors in a leather boat, another undertaken in a wooden boat to a series of islands, including one inhabited by giant smiths, another consisting of a crystal pillar. The island inhabited by giant smiths is probably the volcanic Iceland, while the crystal pillar is

most likely a massive iceberg. While this voyage has some such physi-
cal and historical underpinning, in other words, it draws upon the earlier *imramma* for much of its imagery, so that 'Bran' and 'Brandan' are
versions one of the other. And while they're based largely on pre-
Christian elements, the *imramma* themselves include Christian inter-
polations and borrowings and bleedings-through, including the
mention in *Imram Curaig Maíle Dúin* of bringing back a 'piece of silver
that weighed two ounces and a half' from the net they find on the
island of the immense silver pillar and laying it 'on the high altar of
Armagh'.[40] This 'silver' is picked up by Joyce in 'The Dead' in several
ways. There's the giving of the cabman a silver 'shilling over his fare',
which also brings in the central taboo in *Imram Curaig Maíle Dúin*
involving anything 'extra' in the idea of '*over* his fare'. The element of
the 'excessive' in financial matters extends to 'the sottish Malins' and
the 'pound' Gabriel lent him 'at Christmas, when he opened that little
Christmas-card shop in Henry Street'. This double use of 'Christmas'
emphasizes the Christian veneer of *Imram Curaig Maíle Dúin*, while the
*Mal* in 'Malins' itself brings to mind the *Mael* in Mael Duin. The phrase
'the sottish Malins, also includes a crypto-current, a near version of
'the S(c)ottish Malin', Malin Head being the most northerly point in
Ireland, with a clear view of both Scotland and Tory Island. It's from
Tory Island that a central character in *Imram Curaig Maíle Dúin* hails.
He's another Christian interpolation, the only surviving monk, a cook,
from the group led by another of those seventeen Brendans, St
Brendan of Birr. He's described as being 'very old, so old that he was
covered all over with long, white hair, which grew from his body'. He's
been guilty of selling food meant for the monks, and buying 'many
choice and rare things with the money'.[41] I'm pretty sure that Joyce has
in mind the career of Sir Thomas Gresham, the sixteenth-century
merchant banker after whom Gresham's law, 'bad money drives good
money out of circulation', is named, when he introduces this hermit-
monk as the porter in the *Gresham* Hotel. This porter is, if you recall,
'an old man . . . dozing in a great hooded chair in the hall'. This '*hooded*
chair' emphasizes his monk-like aspect. He carries an 'unstable candle', which Gabriel won't allow him to leave on 'the toilet-table'. This
candle is not, therefore, a stable candle, as would be appropriate to the

*stable*-born Christ, 'the light of the world', and Gabriel resists it being left on the secular 'altar of Armagh', the 'toilet-*table*'. Now let me try to get back to MacNeice, and try to shed a little light on one or two of his most famous poems, beginning with 'Snow'. Written in January 1935, 'Snow' is a poem about simultaneous abuttal and rebuttal:

> The room was suddenly rich and the great bay-window was
> Spawning snow and pink roses against it
> Soundlessly collateral and incompatible:
> World is suddener than we fancy it.
>
> World is crazier and more of it than we think,
> Incorrigibly plural. I peel and portion
> A tangerine and spit the pips and feel
> The drunkenness of things being various.[42]

The discrepancy the speaker of the poem will delineate in the last line ('There is more than glass between the snow and the huge roses') is a version of—what else?—a *féth fiada*. And it derives, at least partly, from the end of 'The Dead', if for no other reason than an Irish writer writing about 'snow' that's not exactly snow, 'snow' at a 'window' that may be the product of a 'fancy', could scarcely be unaware of it. This 'fancy' is a clue to the provenance of the central idea of 'Snow', I think. For it comes from Keats's 'Fancy', a poem in which he writes of a 'faggot' that 'blazes bright', a poem in which he uses the word 'bubbles' twice. This is carried over into MacNeice's 'Snow' as 'And the fire flames with a bubbling sound'. The fire flames because of a 'tangerine', a word that includes a Keatsian pulp and palpability. In 'Fancy', indeed, he writes of both 'caked snow' and 'Autumn's red-lipp'd fruitage too, | Blushing through the mist and dew | cloys with tasting', a paraphrase of 'I feel the drunkenness of things being various'. At the core of 'Fancy', moreover, are these four lines:

> She will bring, in spite of frost,
> Beauties that the earth has lost;
> She will bring thee, all together,
> All delights of summer weather.[43]

MacNeice's poem is not only influenced by Keats's 'Fancy' and Joyce's 'The Dead' but influences Elizabeth Bowen's 'The Tommy Crans', which ends, if you recall, with the image of a couple 'turned back to face the window . . . here and there pink leaflets fluttered into the dark'. I think the 'pink' of those 'pink leaflets' comes directly from MacNeice's 'pink roses'. Not that the MacNeice/Bowen influence was a one-way street. I was delighted to learn, for example, from Jon Stallworthy's biography that MacNeice considered sending his son, Dan, to stay at Bowen's Court during the war, presumably at Elizabeth Bowen's suggestion, while in 1952 he bought 2 Clarence Terrace, the house in London previously occupied by the selfsame Elizabeth Bowen. Bowen and her work, specifically her wartime stories, feed into the next poem of MacNeice I'll consider, his 1961 masterpiece 'The Taxis':

> In the first taxi he was alone tra la,
> No extras on the clock. He tipped ninepence
> But the cabby, while he thanked him, looked askance
> As though to suggest someone had bummed a ride.[44]

Someone *has* 'bummed a ride', of course, in the sense that 'The Demon Lover' who was at the wheel of the cab in Bowen's story becomes 'incorrigibly plural' here, underscoring the speaker's own fractured self. A version of Bowen's driver/guide appears in several of MacNeice's later poems, notably 'Charon', in which the speaker's introduced to the ferryman by a London bus-conductor. He also appears in a slightly earlier poem, 'Hold-Up', a poem about a London traffic jam, in which 'a tall glass box | On the pavement held a corpse in pickle' and 'the conductress | Was dark and lost, refused to change'.[45] The poem immediately preceding this in the *Collected Poems* is 'Reflections', which draws on both 'The Demon Lover' ('she went to the mirror . . . and was confronted by a woman of forty-four') and 'The Tommy Crans' ('The room where they all sat seemed to be made of glass . . . the table was in the window') where MacNeice imagines 'a taxi perhaps will drive in through the bookcase'.[46] The 'No *extras* on the clock' and the idea that 'someone had *bummed a ride*' are likely to derive from MacNeice's sense of the taboos on supernumeracy in *Imram Curaig MaEile DEuin*, which MacNeice must have been reading in 1961, since he proposed the programme idea of *The*

*Mad Islands* in September of that year. The basic narrative of 'The Taxis' also connects it to the cab ride in not only 'The Dead' but, I want to suggest, MacGreevy's *'Crón Tráth na nDéithe'*, a poem which ends with a mimetic breakdown:

> Molly Malone
> And cabs
> And me
> Merely multiple
> In the wet night.
>
> How long?
> How long?
> How long since
> Long till?
>
> Long
>
> Trot
>
> Tr . . .[47]

It seems to me that the 'Merely multiple' is a prefiguring of the 'multiple' personalities of the speaker of 'The Taxis', while the nonsense refrain 'tra la' is prefigured in the 'Tr . . .' of the last line of *'Crón Tráth na nDéithe'*. As we know, MacGreevy's poem was written in 1925, though not published until 1929. I think MacNeice knew it in 1934, the year before he wrote 'Snow', with its 'incorrigibly plural' an extension of MacGreevy's 'Merely multiple', because of a phrase he uses in the poem that comes immediately before 'Snow' in the *Collected Poems*. The poem's called 'Aubade', in which the speaker answers his own question, 'What have we after that to look forward to?' with:

> Not the twilight of the gods but a precise dawn
> Of sallow and grey bricks, and newsboys crying war.[48]

As we know, the phrase 'the twilight of the gods' is a direct translation of *'Crón Tráth na nDéithe'*. I think MacNeice is conscious, also, of the procedures of MacGreevy's 'Homage to Hieronymus Bosch' in a number of the poems in his last, posthumous book, *The Burning Perch*. The movement of 'Hieronymus Bosch', which begins with the nightmarish 'A woman with no face walked into the light; | A boy, in a brown-tree norfolk suit, | Holding on | Without hands | To her seeming skirt' proceeds through such images as 'the group of shadowy figures' and 'the nursery governor flew up out of the well' to 'the woman with no face gave a cry and collapsed' and 'The nursery governor flew back into the well | With the little figure without hands in the brown-tree clothes.'⁴⁹ These are images that would not seem out of place in almost any of those last poems of MacNeice that Edna Longley has so memorably described as 'nightmare nursery-rhymes'.

## Moryson

On the subject of the Sovranty of Ireland, 'the woman with no face', I offer without comment an extract from an account by Fynes Moryson (1566–1630), of his journey through Ulster in late 1602, in the aftermath of the Battle of Kinsale and the Elizabethan conquest of Ireland:

[They] saw a most horrible Spectacle of three Children (whereof the eldest was not above ten Years old,) all eating and gnawing with their Teeth the Entrails of their Mother, upon whose Flesh they had fed 20 Days past, and having eaten all from the Feet upward to the bare Bones, roasting it continually by a slow Fire, were now come to the eating of her said Entrails in like sort roasted, yet not divided from the Body, being as yet raw.⁵⁰

## Ni Chonaill

This startling image has something of its literary counterpart in an episode from *Caoineadh Airt Uí Laoghaire*, the long poem by Eibhlín Dubh Ní Chonaill (c.1745–?). Eibhlín Dubh is not only a woman with no face, but a woman with virtually no dates. We do know that in 1767 she met Art O'Leary, a young man who had fought in the service of Hungary and, though her family disapproved, they married. When Art O'Leary quarrelled with Abraham Morris, the High Sheriff of Macroom, Morris outlawed him, claiming that, under the Penal Laws, a Catholic was not allowed to own any mount worth more than five pounds. It seems that on the morning of 4 May 1773, Art set out to shoot Morris, who was forewarned of the plot and sent his bodyguard to hunt him down. Art O'Leary was shot dead later that day, as Eibhlin Dubh would suddenly realize:

> I never dreamt you would die
> Till your horse came back to me
> With long reins trailing,
> Your blood on its brow
> And your polished saddle
>
> Empty. I started up quickly.
> One leap from the settle,
> The next to the lintel,
> A final fling as far as the stirrup.
> I went off at full gallop.
>
> I would find you stretched
> By that low whin bush
> Without pope or bishop,
> Without priest or monk
> To preside or pray over you,
>
> But some withered old woman
> Who had wrapped you in her mantle.
> Your blood was flowing still,
> I knew of no way to staunch it.
> I cupped my hands and drank it.

This ritualized keening involving the drinking of blood by Eiblin Ni Chonaill is routinely seen as one of the most shocking moments in Irish literature. The other figure in this tableau, this *pietà*, is routinely overlooked but is of course partly the Sovranty of Ireland, the hag in her cloak, partly the *bean nighe* or 'washer woman', versions of whom we've met in Ferguson's Washer at the Ford and, more familiarly, in the hand-wringing Lady Macbeth. This tableau also appears, however faintly, as a crypto-current in the final scenes of 'The Dead' in which Gretta is repeatedly identified with the *washing* of her hair, while Gabriel catches sight of himself, tellingly, 'as he passed in the way of the cheval-glass'.[51] As is often the case, Joyce signposts his allusion with a slight stylistic awkwardness in the phrase 'in the way', as he prepares us for the horse in the '*cheval*-glass'. And we're sent back immediately to Miss O'Callaghan's earlier comment, 'They say you never cross O'Connell Bridge without seeing a white horse.'[52] The *cailleach*, or 'hag', in 'O'Callaghan' has a particular interest in the O'Connell of 'O'Connell Bridge' because, as Joyce is well aware, Eiblín Dubh Ní Chonaill, wife of Art O'Leary, was an aunt of this same Daniel O'Connell. This accounts for the familiar—familial, even—note Gabriel strikes when 'Good night, Dan, he said gaily'.[53] Gabriel is already connected with O'Connell through the echo of the description of his arrival at the Miss Morkans' annual dance—'a light fringe of snow lay like a cape on the shoulders of his overcoat'[54]—in the description of 'the statue, on which lay patches of snow'.[55] The Art O'Leary figure appears, then, partly in the guise of the ghostly Gabriel, partly in Michael Furey, exposed to the elements, lamented by his lover. Joyce's conglomewriting method brings together both Gretta as crone ('He did not like to say even to himself that her face was no longer beautiful but he knew it was no longer the face for which Michael Furey had braved death')[56] and the Morkan/*Mórrigan* crone ('Poor Aunt Julia! She too, would soon be a shade with the shade of Patrick Morkan and his horse. He had caught that haggard look on her face when she was singing *Arrayed for the Bridal*').[57] This coincidence of the 'hag' in 'haggard' and the song-title *Arrayed for the Bridal* brings me back to 'The Phantom's Frenzy'. I don't think Joyce was familiar with the story as such, but I do think that he was familiar with the general iconography and architecture of the tale, in which a king sleeps with a hag of winter, as Gabriel will shortly sleep with Gretta, and she may yet be renewed as a sun maiden. I'm sustained in this belief by the direct reference, repeated as is Joyce's wont when he wants us not to miss his point, to winter and summer within a few lines of each other in Gretta's memory of the span of her relationship with Michael Furey. 'It was in the winter, she said, about the beginning of winter' is followed by 'I wrote a letter saying I was going up to Dublin and would be back in the summer and hoping he would be better then.'[58] Elsewhere, Gretta gives a variant on her own name when she describes herself as being 'great' with Michael Furey, though this could also be read as her presenting herself as *Mór*, the 'Great Queen' associated with Sovranty and the sun, and related to the *Mórrígan*. Gretta's description of her relationship with Michael Furey—'I was great with him at that time'[59]—may also be read as 'I was *pregnant* with him at that time', underlining her fertility-goddess status. No espellor *mór* so, indeed. This reading, if it has any substance, would certainly suggest an answer to that otherwise unanswered, central question in 'The Dead':

There was grace and mystery in her attitude as if she were a symbol of something. He asked himself what is a woman standing on the stairs in the shadow, listening to distant music, a symbol of.[60]

The answer to the question is, as likely as not, 'The Sovranty of Ireland', particularly when allied to the central notion of the *feis*, 'the feast, or celebration', as it's described in James MacKillop's tremendously useful *Dictionary of Celtic Mythology*, 'especially in honour of, or commemorating, the marriage of a king; this would include a symbolic marriage to a sovereignty figure.'[61] Elsewhere, MacKillop reminds us that the ceremony of kingship 'appears to have comprised two main elements: (a) the libation offered by the bride to her husband, and (b) the coition. Whatever the exact nature of this ceremony, the elements of intoxication and sexuality are unmistakably present.'[62] Joyce combines these two elements with startling economy almost immediately Gabriel and Gretta enter their room in the Gresham, when Gabriel speaks of the 'sottish Malins':

—You know that poor fellow, Malins? He said quickly.
—Yes. What about him?
—Well, poor fellow, he's a decent sort of chap after all, continued Gabriel in a false voice. He gave me back that sovereign I lent him.[63]

Not only does Joyce use the word '*sovereign*' in this critical position, but he underscores Gabriel's sexual arousal. He has just experienced 'a keen pang of lust', while 'he could have flung his arms about her hips and held her still for his arms were trembling with desire to seize her and only the stress of his nails against the palms of his hands held the wild impulse of his body in check'.[64] This description of Gabriel and his view of Gretta points to an aspect of the symbolic marriage, lovingly communicated by Giraldus Cambrensis, having to do with the way in which certain kings would array themselves for their *bridles*:

There are some things which, if the exigencies of my account did not demand it, shame would discountenance their being described. But the austere discipline of history spares neither truth nor modesty. There is in the northern and farther part of Ulster, namely in Kenelcunill, a certain people which is accustomed to appoint its king with a rite altogether outlandish and abominable. When the whole people of that land has been gathered together in one place, a white mare is brought forward into the middle of the assembly. He who is to be inaugurated, not as a chief, but as a beast, not as a king, but as an outlaw, has bestial intercourse with her before all, professing himself to be a beast also. The mare is then killed immediately, cut up in pieces, and boiled in water. A bath is prepared for the man afterwards in the same water. He sits in the bath surrounded by all his people, and all, he and they, eat of the meat of the mare which is brought to them . . . When this unrighteous rite has been carried out, his kingship and dominion have been conferred.[65]

The ghostly 'white horse' on O'Connell Bridge is now fleshed out in Joyce's description of Gretta herself. Gabriel has wanted to 'catch her by the shoulders and say something foolish and affectionate in her ear',[66] just as one would whisper in the ear of a horse. He's proud, of course, 'of her grace and wifely *carriage*',[67] while 'she *mounted* the stairs behind the porter, her frail shoulders curved *as with a burden*, her shirt *girt* tightly about her'. This sentence, emphasizing her being an animal in harness, is followed by 'he could have flung his arms about her hips', with its suggestion of coition *a tergo*, while the phrase 'in check' returns us to the harness imagery, picked up again when Gretta stands before 'a large swinging mirror, *unhooking* her waist'.[68] Again, the calculated awkwardness in the phrase 'unhooking her waist' gives the game away, coupled with Joyce's resisting naming the 'swinging mirror' as the 'cheval-glass' as being overly obvious. Within the next few paragraphs, however, Joyce boldly extends the conventional horse/rider image when he writes 'He longed to be *master* of her strange mood' and 'He longed to cry to her from his soul, to crush her body against his, to *overmaster* her.'[69] One final comment on this use of the motif of the ritual of a king marrying his kingdom, or *feis temrach* as it was known when it occurred at Tara, where the 'flank' of King Aedh Mac Ainmirech was more likely than not to have been pressed against the 'flank' of a horse, has to do with the root of the word *feis*, which is *foaidim*, or *faoidhim*, 'to spend the night with, to sleep with'. When Gabriel lies down beside Gretta, he lies down not only with the Sovranty of Ireland but the memory of the *faoidh* in *Furey*, the night-spender par excellence. Together, Gretta and Michael Furey have come to represent the entire country, a country which, however reluctantly, Gabriel will shortly possess, by which long be possessed.

## O'Rathaille

A few brief observations on the combination of private symbolism and political statement, beginning with that *aisling* by Aodhagan O'Rathaille (1670–1728), to which MacGreevy alludes in 'Crón Tráth na nDéithe', as he does to its best-known translation, by James Clarence Mangan:

The Brightest of the Bright met me on my path so lonely;
The Crystal of all Crystals was her flashing dark-blue eye;
Melodious more than music was her spoken language only;
And glorious were her cheeks, of a brilliant crimson dye.

O'er mountain, moor and marsh, by greenwood, lough and hollow,
I tracked her distant footsteps with a throbbing heart;
Through many an hour and day did I follow on and follow,
Till I reached the magic palace reared of old by Druid art.

There a wild and wizard band with mocking fiendish laughter
Pointed out me her I sought, who sat low beside a clown;
And I felt as though I never could dream of pleasure after
When I saw the maid so fallen whose charms deserved a crown.

Then with burning speech and soul, I looked at her and told her
That to wed a churl like that was for her the shame of shames
When a bridegroom such as I was longing to enfold her
To a bosom that her beauty had enkindled into flames.[70]

I want to suggest that not only the central love triangle between the Brightest of the Bright, the clown/churl, and the speaker are picked up in 'The Dead' but that Joyce alludes quite specifically to the language of Mangan's translation. In that last stanza alone we recognize the image, repeated by Joyce, of the burning soul:

For the years, he felt, had not *quenched his soul* or hers. Their children, his writing, her household cares had not *quenched all their souls'* tender fire.[71]

Gabriel also *'longed* to cry to her from his *soul'*,[72] while he's described
as constantly relating to the brightness, or otherwise, of some light
source so that, later, 'instinctively he turned his back more to the light
lest she might see the *shame* that *burned* upon his forehead'.[73] A version of the churl has already appeared as the porter in the Gresham to
whom Gabriel insists, with another repetition bringing to mind the
repetition in the phrase 'The Brightest of the Bright' itself, 'we don't
want any light. We have light enough from the street'.[74] The combination of Gretta's silence at the end of the story and her 'choking with
sobs', coupled with Gabriel's own 'generous tears', are reminiscent,
moreover, of the last verse of 'The Brightest of the Bright':

> But answer made she none; she wept with bitter weeping,
> Her tears ran down in rivers, but nothing could she say;
> She gave me then a guide for my safe and better keeping,—
> The Brightest of the Bright, whom I met upon the way.

# Pearse

This figure of the Sovranty of Ireland that runs from 'The Hag of
Beare' through the blood-drinking crone in the cloak in *'Caoineadh
Airt Uí Laoghaire'* and the 'maid' in 'The Brightest of the Bright' is pre-
dominant in the work of Patrick Pearse (1879–1916), the poet-activist
who masterminded the 1916 rebellion. His best-known poem, *'Mise
Eire'*—'I am Ireland'—is a dramatic monologue that alludes quite
specifically to 'The Hag of Beare' in both its subject matter—the matter of, and with, Ireland—and its wistful-wearish tone. In *'Bean
tSléibhe ag Caoineadh a Mic'*—'The Mountain Woman Keening Her
Son'—Pearse reworks the central motif of *'Caoineadh Airt Uí
Laoghaire'*. Though he doesn't there pick up on what I described earlier as the *'pietà'* of Art O'Leary's body in the arms of the crone/bride,
Pearse is elsewhere only too conscious of the image of the Christ in
the arms of his mother, the mother being Ireland, the 'pierced' Christ
Pearse himself:

Christmas, 1915
O King that was born
To set bondsmen free,
In the coming battle,
Help the Gael![75]

That the coming battle should be joined at Easter, when Pearse/
Christ might be expected to triumph over death by welcoming it, was
a brilliant piece of timing, one that assured the longevity of the term
'Easter Rising', and gave Pearse an emblematic status as the main
rhetorician of Irish nationalism. I'm referring, of course, to Yeats's
distinction between rhetoric and poetry, one stemming from a quarrel with others, the other from the quarrel with oneself.

## Quarles

The English religious poet Francis Quarles (1592–1644), who lived in
Ireland in 1621–2 (when he was secretary to Archbishop Ussher of
Meath, to whom I'll return later), plays on his own name in the sub-
title to 'The Profest Royalist: His *Quarrell* with the Times; maintained
in three Tracts', printed in Oxford in 1643, in which he holds forth with
terrific aplomb on the Lord Protector:

*Cromwell*, that profest defacer of Churches (witnesse *Peterborough*, and
*Lincolne*, &c.) and Rifler of the *Monuments* of the dead, whose profane
Troopers (if Fame has not forgot to speak a Truth) watered their Horses at
the *Font*, and fed them at the *Holy Table*, that *Cromwell*.[76]

## Rodgers

It seems a long way from the plain speech of such rhetoric to the pied
writing on which I've concentrated here, yet most large, social action
begins in the little, clandestine cell, a secret society with a secret language, through which the identities of the members are revealed or
obscured. I'll end this chapter with a few lines from 'Home Thoughts
from Abroad', a poem by W. R. Rodgers (1909–69) about Ian Paisley:

Hearing, this June day, the thin thunder
Of far-off invective and old denunciation
Lambasting and lambegging the homeland,
I think of that brave man Paisley, eyeless
In Gaza, with a daisy-chain of millstones
Round his neck.

Rodgers goes on to equate Paisley with 'the old giants of Ireland', remarks on how 'in this day and age | We can't really have giants lumbering | all over the place' and concludes:

So today across the Irish Sea I wave
And wish him well from the bottom of my heart
Where truth lies bleeding, its ear-drums burst
By the blatter of his hand-me-down talk.
In fond memory of his last stand
I dedicate this contraceptive pill
Of poetry to his unborn followers,
And I place
This bunch of beget-me-nots on his grave.[77]

Here Rodgers follows up the slip and slide from 'lambasting' to 'lambegging' with another 'nice derangement of epitaphs', as Sheridan's Mrs Malaprop might have put it, in the outrageous pun on 'forget-me-not'. In my final chapter, I'll be looking at aspects of this long tradition of sudden shifts and swervings in the work of Sterne, Swift, and Yeats.

# 4

---

*'Contaygious to the Nile'*

# Sterne

I'LL try, in this final chapter, to give some examples of an urge, as expressed by Amergin, the wonder-born poet of the Milesians, towards a kind of exoticism, the tall tale. It's an extension of the urge towards self-dramatization, often in multiple forms, embodied by Amergin, that we looked at in some detail in 'Alone Tra La'. It coincides with a valorization of obliquity and tangentiality that we've seen in any number of Irish writers. And it seems to coexist with at least two other phenomena. One is the slip and slop of language, a disregard for the line between sense and nonsense, as between the 'contiguous' and the 'contaygious' of my title. A second, related, phenomenon is an almost total disregard for linear narrative and the valorization of what I described earlier as 'veerings from, over, and back along a line, the notions of di-, trans-, and regression', veerings that stem not necessarily from some high-flown, literific or literose impulse but from the tradition of popular song and the street ballad. One can scarcely think of 'di-, trans-, or regression' without a mention of Laurence Sterne (1713–68), the author of that reverie of all reveries, *The Life and Opinions of Tristram Shandy, Gentleman*, published in instalments between 1759 and 1767. Written in response to Locke—an un*lock*ing, one might say, of Locke—*Tristram Shandy* takes to the limit the theory of Locke's 'association of ideas' and the tendency for slip and slop I mentioned earlier, a tendency personified by Doctor Slop himself. Now, we've all heard *ab ovo* that Tristram is the embodiment of the post-trystian *tristium* or *tristesse* of his feckless parents. Less seems to have been made, so far as I can make out, of the much more obvious association with Tristram, or Tristan, doomed with his lover, Isolde, to a series of misadventures and misunderstandings, duplicities and 'deviations from a straight line',[1] as Sterne has it. Just as the conventional story of Tristan and Isolde used a potion, or love draught, as a way of kick-starting the narrative, Sterne uses the 'clock' wound, or unwound, by his father to get things under way, though Tristram does refer to his being 'begot and born to misfortunes;—for my poor mother, *whether it was wind or water*—or a compound of both,—or neither;—or whether it was simply the mere *swell* of imagination and fancy in her'.[2] In other words, some 'sea' comes between Tristram and his mother. This 'clock' is also something that intervenes between two lovers at a critical moment, and is thus reminiscent of the sword lying between Tristan and Isolde that's discovered by her suitor, King Mark of Cornwall. A 'mark' in another sense is a feature of the conventional Tristan and Isolde story, in that Tristan suffers a disfiguring wound in the service of the King, the wound for which he's sent to Ireland to be healed. This appears in *Tristram Shandy* as Tristram's 'nose squeezed as flat as my face' by the midwife. This 'mark' is one of the stronger pieces of evidence brought forward to connect the general European version of the love triangle between Mark, Tristan, and Isolde to an Irish genre of *aithed*, or 'elopement tale', of which the best known is *Tóraigheacht Dhiarmada agus Ghráinne*, 'The Pursuit of Dermot and Grace'. Here the old triangle involves Fionn MacCumhaill, Grainne, and Diarmait Ua Duibne. Diarmait has a particular disfigurement, the *ball seirce,* or 'love spot', on his forehead, that women find irresistible. We see a version of it, by the way, in that story by James Joyce—you know the one—in which Gabriel Conroy is described as follows:

The high colour of his cheeks pushed upwards even to his forehead where it scattered itself in a few formless patches of pale red; and on his hairless face there scintillated restlessly the polished lenses and the bright gilt rims of the glasses which screened his delicate and restless eyes.[3]

I suggest that Gabriel is a version of Diarmait for a reason that's deeply encrypted in the story. It has to do with a subliminal reference, more 'pied' than anything we've come across thus far, to Tory island, the home of the old monk at the end of *Imram Curaig Maíle Dúin*. It occurs at that moment when Gabriel and Gretta stand at the door of the Gresham Hotel, and Gabriel thinks back to the earlier part of the evening:

He had felt proud and happy then, happy that she was his, proud of her grace and wifely carriage. But now, after the kindling again of so many memories, the first touch of her body, musical and strange and perfumed, sent through him a keen pang of lust . . . and, as they stood at the hotel door, he felt that they had escaped from their lives and duties, escaped from home and friends and run away together with wild and radiant hearts to a new adventure.[4]

The key to the 'association of ideas' in Gabriel's mind, and the mind of his maker, begins here with the word 'grace', a translation, as we know, of 'Grainne', itself a name reminiscent of 'Gretta'. The idea that they might have 'escaped', a word used twice, and 'run away together . . . to a new adventure' suggests the *Tóraigheacht* itself. For the word *toraigheacht* means, as we know, 'a pursuit'. The first part of the word comes into the English language as 'Tory', originally 'in the seventeenth century, one of the dispossessed Irish, who became out-laws, subsisting by plundering and killing the English settlers or sol-diers' (*OED*). Joyce is aware, I suggest, of the link between *tóraigheacht* and Tory, and it's precisely because of that he's carried along by a strong crypto-current to the image of the monk from *Tory* island in the very next sentence, 'An old man was dozing in the hooded chair in the hall'. The series of tales involving 'Diarmuid and Grania', includ-ing the story of 'How Diarmuid Got His Love-Spot', are included in Lady Gregory's *Gods and Fighting Men*. At one point in Lady Gregory's retelling, she describes how, in order to escape, 'Diarmuid stood up on a high bough of the boughs of the tree, and he rose with a light leap by the shaft of his spear, and lit on the grass far beyond Finn and the Fianna'.[5] This appears in 'The Dead' as the *'light from the street lamp'* that *'lay in a long shaft'* that Gabriel/Diarmuid points out to Gretta/Grainne, who avails herself of this very mode of transport when she's in the Gresham Hotel:

She turned away from the mirror slowly *and walked along the shaft of light* towards him.[6]

Not only are Gretta and Gabriel linked to Grainne and Diarmait, another version of whose story is included in P. W. Joyce's *Old Celtic Romances*, but they're linked, by Joyce's method of conglomewriting, to Deirdre and Naoise, the lovers in the other great Irish pursuit story, *Longas mac nUislenn*, 'The Exile of the Sons of Uisnech'. Here there's also a love triangle involving an older man, Conchobar Mac Nessa, his nephew Naoise, and the famous Deirdre. When Deirdre is a young woman, she witnesses a man skinning a calf on snowy ground. A raven swoops in and begins drinking its blood. Deirdre declares that she would like a man with hair black as the raven, cheeks red as the calf's blood, a body white as snow. These are picked up by Joyce in his description of Gabriel with 'his *glossy black hair*' and 'the *high colour of his cheeks*',[7] while, as we know, there's no shortage of 'snow' in the story. Two further notes. In one version of the story, told by Sir Samuel Ferguson in 'Deirdre's Lament for the Sons of Usnach', Deirdre lays herself to die on the grave of Naoise:

> Dig the grave both wide and deep,
> Sick I am, and fain would sleep!
> Dig the grave and make it ready,
> Lay me on my true love's body. [8]

In another version, Deirdre is given by the sexually thwarted Conchobar Mac Nessa to another man she hates, Eogan Mac Durthacht, the killer of Naoise. As she rides along on Eogan's chariot one day, she leaps from it, dashing her head against a stone, and so getting her death. This is taken over by Joyce in his strange description of Gabriel's point of view of Gretta. He lingers, if you recall, on 'her *grace* and wifely *carriage*'. The combination of 'grace' and 'carriage' is compounded by Gretta's metaphorically 'dashing her head' against the grave, with its unspoken *stone*, of Michael Furey. Joyce connects the moment of sexual jealousy, as Gabriel/Naoise turns into Conroy/Conchobar, with a bird image ('A thought *flew across* Gabriel's mind') that summons up the raven. Immediately following Gabriel's musing that Gretta might have wanted to go to Galway 'with that Ivors girl . . . to see him perhaps', with the appearance of that *gnomon*-esque:

She looked away from him along the shaft of light towards the window in silence.[9]

This conglomewrites Diarmuid's 'shaft of his spear' with the spear used by Eogan Mac Durthacht to kill Naoise as he welcomes him back to Ireland. The name *Eogan* means 'born of the yew', that *gan* being cognate, like the *gin* in *Amergin*, with *genus*. This prepares the way for an aspect of the story of Deirdre and Naoise that Joyce picks up on, the folk tradition of their being buried side by side, the ever-vile Conchobar Mac Nessa driving two yew stakes into their fresh graves that go on to intertwine like two lovers. This itself intertwines with the 'man of yew', *Fer I*, Michael Furey, who is, as we know, identified quite specifically *as* a tree:

He was standing at the end of the wall *where there was a tree*.[10]

The figures of Furey and Conroy are connected, not only through their relationship with Gretta, but by a very delicate thread involving that specific word, 'delicate'. Gabriel is decribed as having 'delicate and restless eyes'[11] while Michael Furey is described twice within three short sentences as 'very delicate' and a 'delicate boy'.[12] And there's a connection between Naoise / Furey and Deirdre / Miss Ivors, in that Miss *Ivors* is herself a 'yew woman', another Old Irish word for yew being *Ibar*. It turns out, indeed, that 'Ivors' is a mirror image, a rough palindrome, of 'Furey'. The palindrome, which runs in two directions simultaneously, which reads the same backwards and for-wards, might well be a basis for the Celtic motif that Miss Ivors pre-sents on her bosom. It is more likely than not some version of a spiral, or interlocking spirals, perhaps even something along the lines of the loop and twirl of the pattern marked out by Corporal Trim as he flourishes his stick in an attempt to give a sense of freedom, particu-larly freedom from the likes of Widow Wadman:

Now, we know that this looping and twirling is emblematic of the twists and turns of *Tristram Shandy*'s narrative, a subject from which I myself seem to have strayed mightily, in my return to the Irish roots of the Tristan and Isolde story. There's a connection, on a philological level, between the *deir* in Deirdre and the *diar* in Diarmait and the *Tri* in Tristan, all having to do with the English word 'tear', with which they're cognate. It's one of the reasons, by the way, why 'generous *tears* filled Gabriel's eyes' as 'he thought of how she who lay beside him had locked in her heart for so many years that image of her lover's eyes' and 'the *tears* gathered more thickly in his eyes and in the partial darkness he imagined he saw the form of a young man standing under a dripping tree'. [13] But I digress yet again. Let me return to an aspect of the conventional story of Tristan and Isolde that is, I suspect, picked up by Sterne in a somewhat radical way, a way that connects to his representation on the page of the diagram of Corporal Trim's stick. I'm thinking of that signal given by Iseult to Tristan that she's coming to his aid. She was meant to come to Brittany from Cornwall in a ship with a white sail, a sign that she's willing to grant him his wish and heal the wound he's suffered from a poisoned arrow. If she's unwilling to heal him, the sail will be black. The sail is white, but Tristan's wife, also known as Iseult, is jealous of the imminent return of his true love, and tells him it's black. Tristan dies of a broken heart. This imagery is probably taken over from the Greek myth of the return of Theseus after killing the Minotaur, when he forgets to show a white sail as he'd agreed, and his father, Aegeus, throws himself into the sea that will bear his name. I suspect that Sterne carries this over into the images of the completely black pages denoting the accumulation of sighs and signs reading 'Alas, poor Yorick' and the completely white page on which we are invited, as readers, to take it upon ourselves to write of the beauty of Widow Wadman, or those that represent missing chapters from the narrative. The use of such devices no doubt influenced Doctor Johnson in his determining that 'Nothing odd will do long. *Tristram Shandy* did not last.' This charge, had it been made to him, would no doubt have been dismissed by Uncle Toby in his usual manner:

My uncle Toby would never offer to answer this by any other kind of argument, than that of whistling half a dozen bars of *Lillabullero*.—You must know it was the usual channel through which his passions got vent, when any thing shocked or surprised him;—but especially when any thing, which he deemed very absurd, was offered.[14]

A verse or two of *Lilla-* or *Lillibullero* might be in order here:

> Dare was an old prophesy found in a bog,
>     Lilli burlero, bullen a-la
> 'Ireland shall be ruled by an ass and a dog.'
>     Lilli burlero, bullen a-la
> Lero, lero, lilli burlero, lero, lero, bullen a-la,
> Lero, lero. Lilli burlero, lero, lero, bullen a-la.
>
> And now dis prophecy is come to pass,
>     Lilli burlero, bullen a-la
> For Talbot's de dog and James is de ass.
>     Lilli burlero, bullen a-la.

This song, often assumed to be part of an anonymous folk tradition, was written in 1687 by Thomas Wharton, to what seems to have been a pre-existing tune, a tune either composed, or arranged (it's not entirely clear which) by Henry Purcell. You'll remember it, perhaps, as the signature tune of the BBC World Service. It's a catchy little number, a point on which Gilbert Burnet, bishop of Salisbury, elaborates in his *History of His Own Time*, published in 1724:

The whole army, and at last the people, both in city and country, were singing it perpetually. And perhaps never had so slight a thing so great an effect.[15]

The effect to which Bishop Burnet refers is that of contributing partly to the forced abdication of James II, such was the general concern about his conversion to Roman Catholicism and the general resentment of his Roman Catholic policy, which would involve, if you recall, his break with his brothers-in-law, Lords Rochester and Clarendon, Lord Clarendon being Lord-Lieutenant of Ireland. These were, of course, the sons of Edward Hyde, the first earl of Clarendon, a name invoked more than once here over the past few days. The dismissal of Clarendon and Rochester took place in 1687, and was no doubt one of the events that prompted Thomas Wharton to take up his pen.

Another might well have been the decision, that same year, to assign Magdalen College, Oxford for the exclusive use of Roman Catholics. Wharton is wonderfully ebullient in its contempt for both James and his Irish policy. The Talbot who's mentioned here is either Richard Talbot, whom James had appointed Lord Deputy of Ireland, also in 1687, two years after making him earl of Tyrconnell, or his brother, Charles Talbot. I speak of Wharton being 'ebullient', and I'm carrying over some of the associations included in that great refrain to *Lillibullero*—Lilli burlero, bullen a-la—that made it pass the old grey whistle test with such flying colours. There's the subversive, seething 'boil' of *ebulliere* in there, as well as the bravado and bravura of 'bully', a 'bully-boy' originally meaning a 'protector of a prostitute' or 'pimp', while a 'bully-cock' in 1687 would have meant a hat, worn at the angle befitting a pimp. This is not to speak of the association of 'Bullaigh', a word you might remember from Art Mac Cumhaigh's *Aisling Airt Mic Cumhaigh*, the line about '*Bhullaigh is Jane ag glacadh léagsai*', 'Willie and Jane are taking out long lets'. This name '*Bhullaigh*', or 'Willie', would come to take on a special significance for the followers of King William III, Prince of Orange and Nassau, their champion against James II. Because of that association, the 'Lilli' in 'Lilli burlero' would later conjure up the 'orange *lily*', one of the emblems denoting loyalty to William III and much favoured by members of the Orange Order, founded in Loughgall over a hundred years later, in 1795, which is one of the reasons why *Lillibullero* continues to be played, as it was whistled by Uncle Toby, at moments when there's no room for 'any other kind of argument'. Quite apart from all this freight that the refrain carries in English, where it's essentially a nonsense rhyme, it means something quite specific in Irish. 'Bullen a-la', as Wharton must have known, is a corruption of *Baineann an la*, a phrase having to do with taking, or carrying the day. Some version of this phrase had supposedly been used by native insurgents in the great revolt of 22 and 23 October 1641. This revolt was but down by, among others, James Butler (1610–88), twelfth earl of Ormond and Ossory, who would serve as Lord-Lieutenant of Ireland on three separate tours of duty. It was Ormond who, in 1649–50, led Royalist resistance to Oliver Cromwell. One or two things you should know about him. He seems to have been the first person to use the word 'tory' of the 'idle boys' and 'plunderers' operating as high-waymen on Irish roads, many of them being Royalists who refused to give up their arms after 1641. He designed the blueprint of Phoenix Park. He also became Chancellor of this university in 1669. We might remember another 'James Butler' who turns up in *The Life and Opinions of Tristram Shandy, Gentleman* as the one and only Corporal Trim, who muses on the significance or otherwise of a name:

I fought just as well, replied the corporal, when the regiment called me Trim, as when they called me James Butler.[16]

It turns out that this 'James Butler' has fought in Ireland with William III. He was present, indeed, at the siege of Limerick in 1690, where he sustained an injury to his knee, and where he no doubt heard another stirring rendition of *Lillibullero*.

## Swift

That *Lilli* in *Lillibullero* also connects us immediately to the *Lilli*put of Jonathan Swift (1667–1745), a writer to whom Sterne would dearly love to be attached. For *Lilly* may also refer to William Lilly (1602–81), the astrologer who predicted the defeat of the Royalists, attributing it to supernatural causes. Another reading, therefore, of the phrase 'Lilli burlero' would be 'Lilly, *ba léir dó*' or, 'it was clear, or evident, to Lilly'. I'll concentrate here on an aspect of Swift that's far less clear—that's to say his interest in, and engagement with, the Irish language and that particular genre of Irish literature upon which we've already touched, the *immram*, or 'voyage tale', one of which has a central place, I suggest, in *Gulliver's Travels*. It needs to be established, first and foremost, if Swift had any grasp of the Irish language. He himself would seem to suggest that he did, if we're to take at face value his sub-title to 'The Description of an Irish Feast'—'translated almost literally out of the original Irish'. The poem begins:

> O'Rork's noble fare
>    Will ne'er be forgot,
> By those who were there,
>    And those who were not.[17]

This last is, of course, an example of the so-called 'Irish bull', the 'self-contradictory proposition . . . an expression containing a manifest contradiction in terms or involving a ludicrous inconsistency unperceived by the speaker', a phenomenon codified by Maria Edgeworth in her 1802 'Essay on Irish Bulls'. The Irish poem Swift's translating here is *Pléaráca an Ruarcach*, 'O'Rourke's Feast', written by Aodh Mac Gabhráin, or Hugh MacGauran. It's not entirely clear if he himself had a hand in the translation of his own poem, providing Swift with a literal version. Nor is it entirely clear if Swift's translation was subsequently set to music by the great harpist and composer Turlough O'Carolan (1670–1738), or if Swift wrote to the template of music O'Carolan had already written for Mac Gabhrain's Irish version. Even if there's insufficient evidence from this example to determine conclusively if Swift had some sense of Irish vocabulary and syntax, it's clear that he had some sense of some of the effects that writers in Irish employed. In his introduction to his 1983 edition of Swift's *Complete Poems*, Pat Rogers goes so far as to suggest that one of the features that emerges in that edition is Swift's 'increasing use of "Irish" rhymes'.[18] By this Pat Rogers means a 'readiness to rhyme words like "dean" and "gain"' that 'seems to go with a certain "Irishness" of idiom'.[19] This would no doubt extend to the rhyming of 'ale' and 'veal' in

> Come, buy my fine oranges, sauce for your veal,
> And charming when squeezed in a pot of brown ale.
> Well roasted, with sugar and wine in a cup,
> They'll make a sweet bishop when gentlefolks sup.[20]

This comes from his 'Verses Made for the Women Who Cry Apples, etc', a series of street songs written in the style of mongers of apples, asparagus, onions, oysters, and herrings:

> Be not sparing,
> Leave of swearing,
> Buy my herring
> Fresh from Malahide,
> Better ne'er was tried.

This evocation of Malahide seems a very long way from the turbocharged tone of Swift's 'Ode to the Honourable Sir William Temple', a poem written in 1692 or 1693, according to Pat Rogers:

> Shall I believe a spirit so divine
>     Was cast in the same mould with mine?
> Why then does nature so unjustly share
> Among her elder sons the whole estate
>     And all her jewels and her plate?
> Poor we cadets of heaven, not worth her care,
> Take up at best with lumber and the leavings of a fate:
>     Some she binds prentice to the spade,
>     Some to the drudgery of a trade,
> Some she does to Egyptian bondage draw,
> Bids us make bricks, yet sends us to look out for straw.[21]

Those images of the 'lumber and leavings' are picked up with Swift's customary gusto in the aftermath of 'A Description of a City Shower':

> Filths of all hues and odours, seem to tell
> What streets they sailed from, by the sight and smell.

The heroic couplet form that Swift uses throughout the poem is varied only once, in the last three lines of the piece:

> Sweepings from butchers' stalls, dung, guts and blood,
> Drowned puppies, stinking sprats, all drenched in mud,
> Dead cats and turnip-tops come tumbling down the flood.[22]

This interest in 'dung, guts and blood' is most famously evident in the voyeuristic 'The Lady's Dressing Room':

> So things which must not be expressed,
> When plumped into the reeking chest,
> Send up an excremental smell
> To taint the parts from which they fell:
> The petticoats and gown perfume,
> And waft a stink round every room.

The close identification of Swift with this subject matter is underscored by the crypto-current of the combination of *'waft'* and *'stink'*, in which an anagrammatical near version of his name appears.

Thus finishing his grand survey,
The swain disgusted slunk away,
Repeating in his amorous fits,
'Oh! Celia, Celia, Celia shits.'[23]

# Synge

You can imagine the dismay if, rather than merely mentioning those *Swift*ian 'shifts', John Millington Synge (1871–1909) had gone the whole hog and suggested that the women of Ireland *shit*. As we know, the word 'shifts', given to Christy Mahon in the line 'It's Pegeen I'm seeking only, and what'd I care if you brought me a drift of chosen females, standing in their shifts itself, maybe, from this place to the eastern world?'[24] was sufficient to incite a riot in January 1907. I've already talked about the fact that Joyce's 'The Dead' was to some extent a response to the upset caused by *The Playboy of the Western World*. The end of the story, with the vision of 'snow . . . general over Ireland', is the logical extension of the whiteness of 'a *drift* of chosen females, standing in their shifts itself, maybe' found throughout the countryside. Synge himself draws on the general store of eighteenth-century Irish song for these eroticized female images, songs like *An Chuimhin Leat an Óiche Úd?*:

> An chuimhin leat an oiche ud
> Do bhi tu ag an bhfuinneog,
> Gan hata, gan laimhne
> Dhod dhion, gan chasog?
> Do shin me mo lamh chut,
> 'S do rug tu uirthi barrog,
> Is d'fan me id chomhluadar
> No gur labhair an fhuiseog.

> Do you remember that night
> That you were at the window,
> With neither hat, nor gloves,
> Nor coat to shelter you;
> I reached out my hand to you,
> And you ardently grasped it,
> And I remained to converse with you
> Until the lark began to sing?[25]

This translation, by George Petrie, of the last line doesn't entirely represent the double entendre of the word *fuiseog*. It does certainly mean a 'lark', but the first component of it is a term for the vulva, *an phis*. The song continues with a description of a scenario that is all too familiar to us:

> Do you remember that night
> That you and I were
> At the foot of the rowan tree,
> And the night drifting snow;
> Your head on my breast,
> And your pipe sweetly playing?
> I little thought that night
> Our ties of love would ever loosen.

Such coded, or not *too* coded, sexual imagery as the 'lark' and the 'pipe' is part and parcel of the folk-song and ballad tradition, as is an association of the 'west' with 'sexuality'. There are several words in Irish including the idea of the west. The first is *iarthar*, the west. Then there's *thiar*, used adverbially of 'in the west, west, behind, in the rear, on the back, behindhand, late'. Then there are *siar*, a word that implies motion 'westward, back' and *aniar*, meaning 'from the west, eastwards, from behind, from a position of lying down in bed to a position of sitting up' while the phrase *siar is aniar* means 'to and fro'. I think you get my drift. It's no accident that in Douglas Hyde's collection of *The Love Songs of Connacht*, the first song is entitled 'If I were to Go West', while the third begins 'In Ballynahinch in the West'. The fourth, meanwhile, begins 'Beside the Breed in the West'.[26] I think you get my drift. Synge would have been quite conscious of these songs, not only in Hyde's translations, published in 1893, but in their original versions. What Yeats praised in Hyde, in his foreword to *The Love Songs of Connacht*, might even more justifiably be applied to Synge:

This little book . . . was the first book that made known to readers that had no Irish, the poetry of the Irish country people. There had been other translators, but they had a formal eighteenth century style, that took what Dr. Hyde would call the 'sap and pleasure' out of simple thought and emotion. Their horses were always steeds and their cows kine . . . Dr. Hyde's prose translations, printed at the end of the book, are I think even better than his verse ones . . . his imagination is indeed at its best only when he writes in Irish or in that beautiful English of the country people who remember too much Irish to talk like a newspaper.[27]

A recognition by Yeats that Synge might be capable of such 'beautiful English' was presumably what lay behind his encouraging Synge in 1896 to go west, a trip Synge undertook a hundred years ago, in May 1898, when he first visited the Aran islands and embarked on his project of transferring into English something of the syntax and metaphorical shape of the Irish language:

PEGEEN. Well, it'd be a poor thing to go marrying your like. I'm seeing there's a world of peril for an orphan girl, and isn't it a great blessing I didn't wed you before himself came walking from the west or south?

SHAWN. It's a queer story you'd go picking a dirty tramp up from the highways of the world.

PEGEEN. And you think you're a likely beau to go straying along with the shiny Sundays of the opening year, when it's sooner on a bullock's liver you'd put a poor girl thinking than on the lily or the rose?

SHAWN. And have you no mind of my weight of passion, and the holy dispensation, and the drift of heifers I'm giving, and the golden ring?

PEGEEN. I'm thinking you're too fine for the like of me, Shawn Keogh of Killakeen, and let you go off till you find a radiant lady with droves of bullocks on the plains of Meath, and herself bedizened in the diamond jewelleries of Pharaoh's ma. That'd be your match, Shaneen. So God save you now![28]

I must confess that I've never quite been able to warm to the muscle-bound aspect of this writing which, while it's clearly not 'talk like a newspaper', is certainly not like any talk heard in the shebeen or the sheep-stall. The term 'bedizened' is the first clue to the *literary* provenance of much of the writing in *The Playboy*. It comes, I suspect, from George Farquhar's *The Beaux' Stratagem*:

I took him for a captain, he's so *bedizen'd* with lace.[29]

This is, after all, another play set in an inn, involving various degrees of duplicity and deception, including the fact that one character, Foigard, is revealed to be MacShane, 'the son of a bogtrotter in

Ireland' whose 'tongue will condemn [him] before any bench in the kingdom'.[30] That Synge's style should rely just as heavily on literary as documentary sources may be explained by the fact that, coincidentally with his field-trips to the Aran islands between 1898 and 1902, Synge was engaged in two major translation projects, one of *Longes mac nUislenn*, 'The Exile of the Sons of Uisnech', another of tales from Geoffrey Keating's *Foras Feasa ar Éirinn*, commonly known as 'A History of Ireland'.

## Toland

Now I will embark on a brief digression within a digression to consider the history of several manuscripts, including that of *Foras Feasa ar Éirinn*. I want to begin with the case of John Toland (1670–1722), the Donegal-born philosopher who, as you'll recall, devised the term 'pantheism'. His notion of pantheism may be rooted in his interest in native Irish religion, particularly druidism. In his posthumously published 1726 piece on 'A History of the Druids', in which he discusses the Beth-Luis-Nion ogham alphabet, Toland writes of those druids:

They also had many characters signifying whole words like the Egyptians and the Chinese.[31]

This 'like the Egyptians' is yet another expression of some deep need through a number of writers out both to establish an 'other' and immediately connect with it, as in Synge's 'diamond jewelleries of Pharaoh's ma'. Toland is already connected to Synge through an incident involving Synge's ancestor, Bishop Edward Synge, one of several Church of Ireland clerics who had denounced him, in 1697, for his denial of the authority of the priest in *Christianity Not Mysterious*. Swift, indeed, called him the 'great Oracle of anti-Christians'. Now, John Toland was of course a speaker of Irish, and is generally assumed to have helped Dermod O'Connor with his translation of *Foras Feasa ar Éirinn*. Keating's book had been published in 1633. O'Connor's translation was published in 1723. Among the tales included here are two of particular interest, I think. The very first to appear in the collection is *'Dha Chluais Chapaill ar Labhraidh Loingseach'*, the story of a king with horse's ears and cognate with the story of Midas and his ass's ears. (The second story, by the way, is a version of the story of the children of Uisnech, that's to say that story of Deirdre and Naoise.) The other aspect of particular interest here is related to the idea of the king with horse's ears. It has to do with a series of kings or heroes named Eochaid. These occur in different stories as Eochaid Aincheann, Eochaidh Mac Ardghail, Eochaidh mhac Eanna Chinnsealaigh, and Eochaidh Tiormcharna. The common element here, *Eochaid*, means 'horse-rider', the *eoch* element being cognate with *equus*. It occurs in myriad forms in Irish literature, as Eochai, Echuid, Echaid, Echaidh, Eocho, Echid, Eochy, and Eochu. It also occurs, I want to suggest, in that book I mentioned earlier, published in 1726, three years after the appearance of Keating in English, as 'Yahoo'. Having offered us horse-humans in the guise of the Houyhnhnms, Swift presents us with a crypto-current of their opposite image in the vile Yahoos. Another story involving an Irish horse-human, the giant Eochu mac Maireda, is one with whom Swift would almost certainly have been familiar from his sojourns in Loughgall, in the environs of Lough Neagh. It has to do with Lough Neagh being formed after Eochu's giant horse urinates there, the lake then taking its name from Eochu. Swift picks up this image, I suspect, in the passage in chapter 5 of the 'Voyage to Lilliput' when Gulliver urinates on the fire in the Queen's apartment:

I voided in such quantity . . . that in three minutes the fire was wholly extinguished, and the rest of that noble pile, which had cost so many ages in erecting, preserved from destruction.[32]

It's because of this urination episode that Gulliver is forced to leave Lilliput, despite the fact that he's a *Nardac*. The narrator describes this as a 'high title',[33] which indeed it is. The *árd* element means 'high' in Irish. The *ac* is another version of the horse-component in Eochaidh, putting Gulliver on a high horse indeed. The other legend associated with Lough Neagh, one upon which Macpherson would draw in his *Ossian* (1760), is that of the giant Fionn

MacCumhaill picking up a sod with which to attack a Scottish rival. The spot from which he pulls up the sod becomes Lough Neagh, the sod itself becomes the Isle of Man. Again, I think something of this is carried over into a tale of shifting scales, a tale of alliances and alienations. I want to suggest that the complex contradictions Swift so brilliantly addresses are evident in Gulliver's name. I've never been particularly persuaded by the contention that Gulliver is a near version of 'gullible', or, at least, never persuaded that that's the end of the story. The first element, 'Gull' is, I suggest, a version of *gall*, the Irish word for a 'foreigner' or 'stranger', of which Swift would have been aware, again if only from that place name Lough*gall*. The second component, 'iver', we recognize yet again from the dreaded Miss Ivors as a version of Eber, one of the sons of the *Mil Espain* after whom Hibernia is named. I know that, once again, I seem to be going out on a bit of a limb here, but I want to suggest that Swift would more likely than not have been aware of the name 'Eibhear' from a very specific source. This was a text called 'The Kings of the Race of Eibhear', which had been translated into English verse by Michael Kearney from the Irish of Sean Mor O Dubhagain in 1635, nearly ninety years before *Gulliver's Travels*. Gulliver is therefore hard-wired, as it were, to simultaneously embody both attachment and estrangement. Now let me reattach myself to John Toland, from whom I've recently become estranged, but to whom I will now return if only because of 'the incessant Revolution of beings and forms' identified by Toland himself in that 'History of the Druids'.[34] In 1694, Toland had met in Oxford with Edward Lhuyd, the Welsh scholar who was then keeper of the Ashmolean Museum, who had already concluded that there was an 'affinity' between the Welsh and Irish languages. This was the selfsame Edward Lhuyd who would visit Ireland in 1699–1700 under the auspices of the Dublin Philosophical Society, where he acquired a number of the fascicle-manuscripts of such stories as 'The Destruction of Da Derga's Hostel', 'The Cattle Raid of Cooley', 'The Exile of the Sons of Uisliu', and 'The Voyage of Mael Duin's Currach', and compiled them into what we now know as *The Yellow Book of Lecan*.

# Ussher

There had of course been a tradition of collecting manuscripts before the arrival of Edward Lhuyd. I think particularly of James Ussher (1581–1656), who moved from being Professor of Divinity at Trinity College, Dublin, in 1607 to an appointment as Bishop of Meath in 1621 to the Archbishopric of Armagh in 1625. The Bishopric of Meath, I'm reminded by R. Buick Knox, on whose study of *James Ussher, Archbishop of Armagh*,[35] I'm drawing for these details, is based at Trim, a village near which Swift also briefly had a living in 1700. The name is carried over by Sterne as Corporal *Trim*. You'll recognize the crypto-current of Ussher's own name from *Usher*'s Island, the location for that story by James Joyce, from which a cabman is exhorted to 'make like a bird for Trinity College'.[36] James Ussher's vast library, which he had built on behalf of Trinity College, was seized by Oliver Cromwell and returned to Trinity only after the Restoration of Charles II. *Oliver* Cromwell. That *Oliver* in Oliver Cromwell is surely a near version of 'Gulliver', a man who takes a country by storm, leaving piles of dead in his wake, just as I'm about to storm through the next couple of letters of the alphabet. If you're wondering what I'm going to do when I get to X, so am I.

# Vallancey

The work of collecting manuscripts undertaken by Ussher was expanded by a succession of antiquarians, one of the most important of whom was General Charles Vallancey (1721–1812), an English soldier who had come to Ireland in 1762. Within ten years he would found a journal, *Collectanea de Rebus Hibernicis*, focusing on all manner of Irish matters. In 1779 Vallancey would be instrumental in setting up the Hibernian Antiquarian Society, while in 1782 he would play a key role in founding the Royal Irish Academy. Among his many interests was the ogham tree-alphabet, the study of which he pioneered in a 1785 essay on 'The Callan Stone'. He had a wonderfully wacky take on comparative linguistics (where have you come across *that* lately?) that had him trace the origins of Irish to the language of the Phoenicians. I quote from 'An Essay on the Antiquity of the Irish Language with a Collation of the Irish with the Punic Language' which was first published in at least 1772. (I'm using an 1822 text which includes an admiring response to Vallancey's theory dated 1772 by a correspondent who signs himself 'Celticus'.) Here Vallancey compares and contrasts a 1482 edition of the *Poenulus* of Plautus held by the library of Trinity College 'from which the Punic speech is transcribed, together with the Latin translation'.[37] Vallancey first gives an example of what Plautus offers as Phoenician:

> *Nyth al o nim ua lonuth sicorathissi me com syth*
> *Chim lach chumyth mum ys tyal mycthii bari schi*

This is rendered in Irish as:

> *N'iaith all o nimh uath lonnaithe! Socruidhse me con sith!*
> *Chimi lach chuinigh! Muinigh is toil, miocht beiridh iar mo scith.*

Vallency appeals to the parallel text in Latin:

> *Deos deasque veneror, qui hanc urbem colunt ut quod de mea re*
> *Huc veneri te venerim. Measque ut gnatas et mei fratris filium*
> *Reperirem.*

This substantiates, supposedly, the rendition into English:

> Omnipotent much dreaded Deity of this country! asswage my
>     troubled mind,
> Thou the support of feeble captives! being now exhausted with
>     fatigue, of my free will guide me to my children.[38]

## Wilde

Before I embark on one or two suggestions which, I trust, won't quite partake of the valency of Vallancey, I'll continue with this digression within a digression within a digression to mention Sir William Wilde (1815–76). Wilde is relevant here for at least two reasons. The first has to do with his work as a doctor, particularly his account of *The Closing*

*Years of Dean Swift's Life*, his 1849 diagnosis of Swift's succumbing to
Ménière's disease, rather than madness. The second has to do with his
continuation of the work begun by Vallancey at the Royal Irish
Academy. It was Wilde, for example, who in 1862 put together the
complete catalogue of the holdings of artefacts of the RIA, including
the intricately scrolled Tara Brooch, almost certainly the model for
Miss Ivors's neck-bodkin. The RIA now also had a huge manuscript
collection, including *Lebor na hUidre*, 'The Book of the Dun Cow',
which contained the main version of *Immram Brain*. This manuscript
had, in 1837, come into the possession of a Dublin bookseller by the
name of George Smith. In 1470, it seems, it had been part of the booty
picked up by Red Hugh O'Donnell after a long siege of Sligo Castle.
So far as I can make out, no one knows the precise whereabouts of
'The Book of the Dun Cow' between 1470 and 1837.

# The 'X' Factor

Such an 'X' factor leads me to ponder one or two other imponder-
ables. I've already touched on our imprecise sense of how much Irish
Swift might have known. We do know that in *The Drapier's Letters* he
at least *seems* to take a less than supportive view of the fact that the
Irish have the habit of speaking the Irish language. In 'An Humble
Address to Parliament' Drapier advises

That some effectual Methods may be taken to civilize the poorer Sort of our
Natives, in all those parts of this Kingdom where the Irish abound; by intro-
ducing among them our Language and Customs; for want of which they live
in the utmost Ignorance, Barbarity and Poverty; giving themselves wholly up
to Idleness, Nastyness and Thievery.[39]

It's hard to know to what extent this truly represents Swift's attitude
either to the Irish or their language, particularly when it was written in
1723, during the period he was working on *Gulliver's Travels*. It's difficult
to determine, in other words, the extent to which his view might be
'Erinized', along with his complex view of the Yahoos, also notable for
their 'Ignorance, Barbarity and Poverty' not to speak of their 'Idleness,
Nastyness and Thievery'. I've suggested that the provenance of the

word 'Yahoo' might derive from *Foras Feasa ar Éirinn*, as indeed might the 'Gull' in Gulliver, since Keating makes much of the distinction between the '*Nua-Ghaill*', the 'New Foreigners' and the '*Sean-Ghaill*' or 'Old Foreigners'. We know that it was translated into English in 1723, the year Swift wrote that 'Humble Address to Parliament'. For a while I was excited by the fact that Swift might also have read the 1660 translation into Latin of *Foras Feasa ar Éirinn*, made by John Lynch, until I discovered it was never actually published. This John Lynch, though, is an interesting fellow. He was born in Galway in about 1599 and was a student of one Dubhaltach Mac Fir Bhisigh. This Dubhaltach Mac Fhir Bhisigh is another very interesting fellow. He was born in about 1600 in Lackan, County Sligo, a place we might recognize as the provenance of that *Yellow Book*. It was indeed an ancestor of Dubhaltach Mac Fhir Bhisigh, Giolla Iosa Mac Fhir Bhisigh, who compiled the book in or around 1392. It was Dubhaltach Mac Fhir Bhisigh who met, sometime in 1669–70 with that other extremely interesting fellow, Edward Lhuyd, and is more likely than not the person who gave Lhuyd the manuscripts that would become *The Yellow Book of Lecan*. Mac Fhir Bhisigh was also friendly with a very, very interesting fellow called Sir James Ware, who'd hired him, in 1665–6, to translate and transcribe Irish manuscript material on his behalf. That manuscript collection, by the way, would be the basis for the Clarendon collection in the Bodleian. Now, this Dubhaltach Mac Fhir Bhisigh was also friendly with a very, very, very interesting fellow called Roderick O'Flaherty, one of his former students and author of *Ogygia* (1685), a chronology of Irish history written in Latin. Taking its title from Plutarch's name for an island west of Britain, it includes a reference to Hy-Brasil, the fabulous land even further west. This Roderick O'Flaherty not only met with Edward Lhuyd in 1670 but was friendly with two very, very, very, very interesting fellows by the names of Sean and Tadhg O'Neachtain, the centre of that enthusiastic group of scholars and scribes who included that very, very, very, very, very interesting fellow by the name of Aodh Mac Gabhrain, author of 'O'Rourke's Feast', translated by that other interesting fellow. What I'm getting at here is that Swift was familiar with the extended circle of Irish scholarship that flourished in late seventeenth- and early eighteenth-century

Dublin. Sean O'Neachtain's main patron, for example, was Anthony Raymond, a friend of Swift, who served as Vicar of Trim in 1705, a mere five years after Swift had been there himself. Swift recommended him for appointment as chaplain to Charles Talbot, brother of Richard, in 1713. Back in 1699, when Raymond had been elected a Fellow of TCD in 1699, Swift was also in Dublin, serving as chaplain to the Earl of Berkeley. It may even be that Swift met Edward Lhuyd in that 1699–70 period, given the circles in which he was already beginning to move. Again, what I'm driving at is that Swift is more likely than not to have been influenced by a text collected by Lhuyd and with which the circle in which he moved was quite familiar. That text is *Imram Curaig Maíle Dúin*, that voyage tale to which I've already paid rather a lot of attention. We accept only too readily that Swift drew upon the *Odyssey*, Plato's *Republic* (for Atlantis), Lucian's *True History*, More's *Utopia*, Cyrano de Bergerac's *Journey to the Moon*, Rabelais's *Voyage of Pantagruel*, Defoe's *Robinson Crusoe*. My evidence for adding *Imram Curaig Maíle Dúin* to this list has to do primarily with two names. We know very well of Swift's interest in names and puns on names, including his own. I want to suggest that the name 'Lemuel' is a near version, a virtual anagram, of that *Maíle* in the title of *Imram Curaig Maíle Dúin*. There are several other names of characters in *Gulliver's Travels* that have such an anagrammatical quality. One is 'Reldresal', which sounds to me like a combination of elements of *El Dorado* and a near version of Roderic O'Flaherty's Hy-Brasil. Then there's 'Bolgolam'. The first element here, *bolg*, is the Irish word for 'belly'. We've seen it in the *Fir Bolg*, one of the groups of mythical invaders of Ireland, their name cognate with the *Belgae*. The second element, *lam*, means 'hand'. We've seen it in the name *Lugh Lamhfhada*, 'Lugh of the Long Hand'. As we know, *Lugh* is an emissary, a go-between, and that aspect of him is embodied in the reversal of *Lug* in the *Gul* of 'Gulliver', the ultimate shuttle diplomat. *Lugh* also appears in the name 'Lustrog', the great prophet of Lilliput. And let us remind ourselves of the name of the capital city of Lilliput. It is 'Mildendo', as clear an allusion as one could hope to find to the *Maeile Dúin* of *Imram Curaig Maíle Dúin*. Just in case we miss it there, Swift gives it to us again, in the city of 'Maldonada', pointing up its significance the first time we come upon the word with the phrase '(for so it is called)'.[40] It's from Maldonada that Lemuel Gulliver sets sail for 'Luggnagg'—there's *Lugh* again—and 'Glubbdubdrib', the etymology of which place name Gulliver takes the trouble to gloss:

Glubbdubdrib, as far as I can interpret the word signifies the Island of Sorcerers or Magicians.[41]

Swift is sending us a clear signal here that he is engaged by a specifically Irish etymology, since the 'dri' element in Glubbdubdrib is a version of *draoi*, the Irish word from which 'druid' derives, itself stemming from the *duir*, or sacred 'oak tree' with which I introduced Amergin in the first of these talks. The 'dub' is a clear allusion to the 'Dub' of *Dub*lin, while the 'lin' aspect of that name has already been picked up twice in 'Lindalino', the scene of a recent rebellion. In his description of the attempt by the King of Laputa to put down that rebellion, Swift is no doubt thinking of the Rebellion of 1641 as it affected Dublin, when Sir John Temple, brother of his patron, Sir William, was quartermaster for the city. The first element in the Irish name for Dublin, *Báile Átha Clíath*, is reflected in 'Balnibarbi', though the second is a version of the 'barbarity' that Drapier noted among the natives of Ireland. The *Baile* element is reflected in the mirror-written or semi-palindromic aspect of the first element of '*Glubb*dubdrib', though *bulg* is not only a mirror-version of the aforementioned *Bolg* but includes the name *Lugh*. This tendency toward the palindromic leads me back to Edward Lhuyd (his own name cognate with *Lugh*, I'd say), and a complaint made of his transcription skills by General Vallancey in his essay 'On The Antiquity of the Irish Language':

Mr. Lhwyd [sic] has done a great injustice to the original, as he did not understand our *Cionn fa eite* or *Cor fa chasan* i.e. *Boustrophedon* of the Irish; and has consequently made a great jumble of unconnected words.[42]

This convention of turning round as in 'the top of the ridge' or 'the reaper's path' or the 'ox-turning' in writing from line to line, regressing as it were, is central to an understanding of Swift's method in his use of these Irish elements in *Gulliver's Travels*, a story about a man who cannot, like Mael Duin, bring himself to recognize his own humanity. A footnote on Edward Lhuyd. When he died, in 1709, his manuscript collection, including the manuscript of *Imram Curaig Maíle Dúin*, was impounded by Oxford University so as to pay off his considerable debts. (These manuscripts were bought, it seems, by Sir Thomas Sebright in 1715, and were returned by his son, Sir John Sebright, to the library of Trinity College Dublin in 1786, at the suggestion of Edmund Burke.)

At this point, I need to pay off some of my own considerable debts, beginning with the Oxford University Department of English and Oxford University Press, particularly in the persons of Nigel Smith, Sophie Goldsworthy, and Matthew Hollis. I also want to thank Wadham College, and especially Bernard O'Donoghue, for affording me hospitality over the ten days or so in which these lectures were given. I want to thank also some of my colleagues at Princeton— Michael Cadden, James Richardson, and P. Adams Sitney—who were kind enough to read early drafts of the lectures. Finally, I want to thank you for being such a generous, good-humoured audience as I've fumbled around this massive subject.

## Yeats

The work of W. B. Yeats (1865–1939) is a massive subject in itself, one to which I hope to return. I propose here to look very briefly at two or three aspects of Yeats, beginning with his handling of the story of Deirdre and Naoise in *Deirdre*, a play first produced in November 1906. Yeats's main source is generally acknowledged to be Lady Gregory's retelling of the tales associated with *Cuchulain of Muirthemne* in the book of that title, published in 1902, which he'd praised, with all his usual pomposity, as 'the best that has come out of Ireland in my time'.[43] Yeats had almost certainly been familiar with the story of Deirdre and Naoise from P. W. Joyce's *Old Celtic Romances* (1879) since at least 1888, when he mentions Joyce in letters to Douglas Hyde and John O'Leary[44] and, some months later, writes to Joyce for advice on a Gaelic song.[45] But I suspect Yeats was also familiar with the *Deirdre* of Robert Dwyer Joyce (brother of P. W.), published in 1877, if only because of the dramatic device of the game of chess which Yeats borrows from the section Joyce entitles 'Tragedy of the Red Branch' with its description of the death of Maini presented in not-too-shabby couplets:

> He prowled around the Red Branch, till he found
> An unshut window full of light and sound
> From the great hall and, peering through, his eye
> Marked Deirdre and her husband silently
> Moving the chessmen still, their little son
> Beside them laughing. Suddenly as one,
> Dreaming of danger, wakes with hurried glance,
> And sees the foeman night with threatening lance,
> Deirdre, instinctive, laid her chessman down,
> And looked and saw the swarth face and the frown
> Outside the window, and with secret word
> Told Naisi, who a chessman from the board
> Took, poised, and threw with swift unerring aim,
> And struck, uprooting Maini's eye of flame
> Out of its bleeding orbit![46]

As well as using the chess-game as a dramatic device, Yeats picks up R. D. Joyce's 'swarth face' in a 'Dark-faced Messenger' who comes to the doorway, one of those many 'dark-faced men' who will later drag in Naoise 'in a net' and crowd round Conchubar, Conchubar who comments that

> One woman and two men; that is the quarrel
> That knows no ending.[47]

Let me digress yet again to suggest that our friend James Joyce conglomewrites both R. D. Joyce's *Deirdre* and Yeats's *Deirdre* into the fabric of 'The Dead', his own meditation of 'one woman and two men', including that shared, central image of the chessboard, which Joyce presents as the dinner table itself:

A fat brown goose lay at one end of the table and at the other end . . . lay a great ham . . . *Between these rival ends ran parallel lines of side-dishes.*[48]

Joyce extends, if we recall, the chess/warfare imagery with the details of '*sentries* to a fruit-stand' and '*squads* of bottles of stout and ale and minerals, *drawn up according to the colours of their uniforms,* the first two *black,* with brown and red labels, the third and smallest squad *white,* with transverse green sashes'.[49] And Joyce goes back to Joyce, I suspect, for other key images. We've already met in R. D. Joyce the 'unshut window full of light', which blends and bleeds into the windows from which Gretta sees Michael Furey and at which Gabriel sees Gretta while, to respond to the 'uprooting' of 'Maini's eye of flame', Joyce has Freddy *Malins,* his name a near version of 'Maini', 'rub the knuckles of his left fist backwards and forwards *into his left eye'.*[50] A reader may also appeal to R. D. Joyce to make further sense of some details of the landscape of the end of the story. I'm thinking in particular of the connection between the 'vast *hosts* of the dead', the 'spears' and the 'dark *mutinous* Shannon *waves'.* This image-cluster derives partly, I suggest, from these lines in *Deirdre:*

> Again strong Naisi cried his battle-cry,
> And Ainli on his left, and Ardan tall
> On his right hand, through the spear-bristling wall
> Of brass-clad breasts before him thundering drave
> With his fierce *host,* as drives the Barrow's *wave*
> Through the late fields of barley, when the rain
> Pours upon Blama's hills, and rock and plain
> Bellow with autumn storms. So through the foe
> He rushed with his strong *host.*[51]

This is followed only a few lines later by the image of the *'ever-bickering wave',* which also feeds and flows into 'the mutinous Shannon waves'.

I'm likely to see a little insurrection myself, I know, when I suggest that Yeats's *Deirdre* feeds and flows into 'The Dead' since, as I mentioned, the play was first produced in November 1906, while Joyce was in Rome. There's no solid evidence that he'd read it when it was first published in July 1907, but he certainly *could have* read it by the time he finished 'The Dead' in September 1907, however narrow the little window of opportunity. One way or another, there are quite striking parallels between the two texts, especially in the use of 'Three Musicians' ('The Three Graces') who provide a musical commentary—to such an extent, indeed, that their 'sad music' becomes a character in the play in which, as the Musicians put it, Deirdre and Naoise are gone 'into the secret wilderness of their love',[52] leaving Conchubar Mac Nessa 'letting no boy lover take the sway'.[53]

Which brings me round to Louis MacNeice and his perceptive comments, in his ground-breaking study of *The Poetry of W. B. Yeats*, on Yeats's abiding interest in popular song, particularly the ballad tradition and his use of the refrain:

Some poets . . . use the refrain as a rhythmical norm for the whole; this is often so in popular narrative poetry where, the verses being allowed to sprawl in order to accommodate the story, the refrain is used to pull the procession back on the road. A refrain again, when it means anything, tends to be simpler in meaning than the rest of the poem; it gives the reader or hearer relief. Yeats's use of it, therefore, is often in two respects unusual. First the music of his refrain is often less obvious or smooth than that of his verses themselves, being sometimes flat, sometimes halting, sometimes strongly counterpointed. Secondly, his refrains tend to have either an intellectual meaning which is subtle and concentrated, or a symbolist or nonsense meaning which hits the reader below the belt.[54]

MacNeice's phrase 'below the belt' is in itself intriguing, sending a reader in the direction of the bawdy of Swift, so beloved of Yeats. More often than not, though, Yeats is interested in achieving the effect which he described to Frank O'Connor as follows:

You must always write as if you were shouting to a man across the street who you were afraid wouldn't hear you, and trying to make him understand.[55]

This engagement with the 'man across the street' leads Yeats to quote popular songs including, in *Deirdre* itself, the aforementioned 'Do You Remember That Night?':

> Do you remember that first night in the woods
> We lay all night on leaves, and looking up,
> When the first grey of the dawn awoke the birds,
> Saw leaves above us?[56]

It also leads him, in refrain-driven poems like 'The Ghost of Roger Casement', to issue invitations such as:

Draw round beloved and bitter men,
Draw round and raise a shout:

*The ghost of Roger Casement*
*Is beating on the door.*[57]


## Zozimus

This 'draw round', like Yeats's exhortation in 'Come Gather Round
Me Parnellites', comes directly, I suspect, from a poem by Zozimus,
the pseudonym of Michael Moran (?1794–1846), the blind Dublin
ballad-maker, and his famous come-all-ye:

> Gather round me, boys, will yez
>     Gather round me?
> And hear what I have to say
>     Before ould Sally brings me
> My bread and jug of tay.[58]

The most famous piece by this Zozimus is 'The Finding of Moses':

> In Egypt's land, contaygious to the Nile,
> King Pharaoh's daughter went to bathe in style.
> She tuk her dip, then walked unto the land,
> To dry her royal pelt she ran along the strand.
> A bulrush tripped her, whereupon she saw
> A smiling babby in a wad o' straw.
> She tuk it up, and said with accents mild,
> ''Tare-and-agers, girls, which av yez owns the child?'[59]

I quote these versions of 'Gather round me, boys' and 'In Egypt's
Land' from Yeats's essay on 'The Last Gleeman', as he styles Zozimus,
in *The Celtic Twilight*. The name 'Zozimus' derives from Moran's
'Saint Mary of Egypt', a long poem which, according to Yeats, 'told
how an Egyptian harlot, Mary by name, followed pilgrims to
Jerusalem in pursuit of her trade, and there, on finding herself with-
held from entering the Temple by supernatural interference, turned
penitent, fled to the desert and spent the remainder of her life in soli-
tary penance. When at last she was on the point of death, god sent

Bishop Zosimus to hear her confession, give her the last sacrament, and with the help of a lion, whom He sent also, dig her grave.' Yeats would have been particularly taken, I suspect, by the transgression implied in the presenting of 'contaygious' for 'contiguous', given his own regard for the fine line between the two:

> 'A woman can be proud and stiff
> When on love intent;
> But love has pitched his mansion in
> The place of excrement;
> For nothing can be sole or whole
> That has not been rent.'[60]

Those lines are taken from 'Crazy Jane Talks with the Bishop'—is it possible that the 'Bishop' in these poems is *Bishop* Zozimus?—and they owe something, at least indirectly, to the zest of 'A Description of a City Shower', with its 'dung, guts and blood' in the aftermath of the cloudburst:

> Now in contiguous drops the flood comes down,
> Threatening with deluge this devoted town.[61]

I've no evidence to suggest that Zozimus himself had ever heard this poem, or that that's where he came by his cock-eyed 'contiguous'. It's quite likely, however, that he'd have heard such poems as 'The Lady's Dressing Room', which had a long life in pamphlets, newspapers, and broadsides, with its insistence on

> Such order from confusion sprung,
> Such gaudy tulips raised from dung.[62]

The discrepancy between appearance and reality, with which these lectures began, is at the heart of another popular Swift poem, 'A Beautiful Young Nymph Going to Bed':

> Corinna in the morning dizened,
> Who sees, will spew; who smells, be poisoned.[63]

There's that 'dizened' again, which may also form part of Synge's back of the mind in those lines from *The Playboy of the Western World* about 'herself bedizened in the diamond jewelleries of Pharaoh's ma'. These references to 'Egypt' in Synge and Zozimus put them firmly in a line that, despite all its trans-, di-, and regressions, runs 'swiftly asterne', as Joyce has it in *Finnegans Wake*, all the way back to where we started, to *Lebor Gabala Erenn*, 'The Book of Invasions', back to the pseudo-poet Amergin, his brother Eber, to their parents the *Mil Espain* and Scota, daughter of Nectanabes, the great Pharaoh of Egypt.

# Endnotes

## Chapter 1

1. John Montague, *The Faber Book of Irish Verse* (London: Faber, 1974), 44.
2. Robert Graves, *The White Goddess* (New York: Noonday Press, 1948).
3. Ibid. 207.
4. George Russell (AE), *Collected Poems* (London: Macmillan, 1913).
5. Quoted in *The Field Day Anthology of Irish Literature*, xi (1991), 541.
6. *Pairlement Chloinne Tomais*, ed. N. J. A. Williams (Dublin: Institute for Advanced Studies, 1980).
7. Thomas Kinsella (ed. and trans.), *The New Oxford Book of Irish Verse* (Oxford: Oxford University Press, 1986).
8. Gerard Murphy (ed.), *Early Irish Lyrics* (Oxford: Oxford University Press, 1956), 7.
9. Ibid. 157–9.
10. Samuel Beckett, *Krapp's Last Tape* (New York: Grove Weidenfeld, 1958), 22–3.
11. Samuel Beckett, *Molloy, Malone Dies, The Unnamable* (New York: Grove Press, 1955), 37.
12. *Foclóir Gaedhilge agus Béarla*, an Irish–English Dictionary compiled and ed. Revd. Patrick S. Dinneen (Irish Texts Society, 1927).
13. *Molloy, Malone Dies, The Unnamable*, 210–11.
14. James Joyce, *Finnegans Wake* (London: Penguin Books, 1939), 467.
15. *Molloy, Malone Dies, The Unnamable*, 211.
16. *Krapp's Last Tape*, 27.
17. *Finnegans Wake*, 112.
18. Samuel Beckett, *Waiting for Godot* (New York: Grove Press, 1954), 57–8.
19. Murphy (ed.), *Early Irish Lyrics*, 157.
20. *Krapp's Last Tape*, 19.
21. *Molloy, Malone Dies, The Unnamable*, 181.
22. *Waiting for Godot*, 28.
23. *Molloy, Malone Dies, The Unnamable*, 293.
24. Samuel Beckett, *Watt* (New York: Grove Press, 1953), 254.

25. *The Collected Stories of Elizabeth Bowen* (New York: Ecco Press, 1989).

26. 'The Dead', in *The Portable James Joyce*, ed. Harry Levin (London: Penguin, 1976), 190–242.

27. *Krapp's Last Tape*, 26.

28. Seamus O Cathain, *The Festival of Brigit* (Dublin: DBA Publications, 1995).

29. William Carleton, *Father Butler and The Lough Dearg Pilgrim* (Dublin: William Curry, 1829), 201–2.

30. *Selected Joyce Letters*, ed. Richard Ellmann (New York: Viking, 1966), 124.

31. Ibid.

32. Ibid.

33. Ibid. 125.

34. William Carleton, *Traits and Stories of the Irish Peasantry*, i (Dublin: Wakeman, 1833), 125–7.

35. Ibid. 130.

36. Brian Coffey, *Poems and Versions 1929–1990*, ed. J. C. C. Mays (Dublin: Dedalus, 1991), 5–6.

37. *Collected Poems of Denis Devlin*, ed. J. C. C. Mays (Dublin: Dedalus, 1989), 37.

38. Samuel Beckett, under pseudonym of Andrew Belis, *Bookman* (August 1934).

39. *Collected Poems of Denis Devlin*, 133.

40. *Krapp's Last Tape*, 26.

41. *Collected Poems of Denis Devlin*, 135.

42. *Krapp's Last Tape*, 16.

43. Ibid. 22.

44. 'The Dead', 237.

45. Ibid. 241.

46. *Krapp's Last Tape*, 28.

47. 'The Dead', 241.

48. *Collected Poems of Denis Devlin*, 134.

49. Maria Edgeworth, *Castle Rackrent* (1800; repr. New York: W. W. Norton, 1965), p. x.

50. Walter Allen, *The English Novel* (London: Penguin, 1954).

51. John Cronin, *The Anglo-Irish Novel* (Belfast: Appletree Press, 1980), 26.

52. *Molloy, Malone Dies, The Unnamable*, 8.

53. *Watt*, 215.

54. Ibid. 228.

## Chapter 2

1. Shakespeare, *Macbeth*, ed. Sylvan Barnet (New York: Signet, 1963), 70.
2. Arthur Deering, *Sir Samuel Ferguson, Poet and Antiquarian* (Philadelphia, 1931), 104.
3. Sir Samuel Ferguson, *Poems* (Dublin, 1880); id., *Lays of the Western Gael* (Dublin and London: Sealy, Bryers and Walker, 1888).
4. W. B. Yeats (ed.), *A Book of Irish Verse Selected from Modern Writers* (London: Methuen, 1895).
5. W. B. Yeats, *The Bookman* (May 1896), 50.
6. Hugh Walker, *Literature of the Victorian Era* (Cambridge, 1910).
7. Gerald of Wales, *The History and Topography of Ireland*, trans. and with an introduction by John O'Meara (London: Penguin, 1982).
8. Alfred Perceval Graves, 'Has Ireland a National Poet?', *The Reflector* (April 1888).
9. Ibid.
10. R. F. Foster, *W. B. Yeats: A Life* (Oxford: Oxford University Press, 1997), 53.
11. W. B. Yeats, *Dublin University Review* (November 1886).
12. W. B. Yeats, *The Bookman* (May 1896).
13. W. B. Yeats, Introduction to Lady Gregory, *Gods and Fighting Men* (London: John Murray, 1904; Dublin: Colin Smythe, 1970).
14. Lady Gregory, *Gods and Fighting Men*, 87.
15. 'The Colony', in *The Selected John Hewitt*, ed. with an introduction by Alan Warner (Belfast: Blackstaff Press, 1981), 21–4.
16. Lady Ferguson, *Sir Samuel Ferguson in the Ireland of His Day* (London: W. Blackwood, 1896), i. 262–6.
17. Ibid.
18. Douglas Hyde, 'The Necessity for De-Anglicizing Ireland' (1892).
19. Ibid.
20. Standish O'Grady, *History of Ireland: Critical and Philosophical* (London: Sampson Low / Ponsonby, 1881).
21. John O'Donovan, quoted in Don Gifford, *Ulysses Annotated* (Berkeley & Los Angeles: University of California Press, 1988), 211.
22. James Joyce, *Dubliners*, collected in *The Portable James Joyce*, ed. Harry Levin (London: Penguin, 1947).
23. James Joyce, quoted in Herbert Gorman, *James Joyce* (New York: Farrar, 1939), 150.
24. John V. Kelleher, 'Irish History and Mythology in James Joyce's "The Dead" ', in *The Review of Politics* (1964), 414–33.

25. 'The Dead', in *The Portable James Joyce*, 213.
26. Ibid. 203.
27. Stanley Sultan, *Eliot, Joyce and Company* (Oxford: Oxford University Press, 1987).
28. Maria Tymoczko, *The Irish Ulysses* (Berkeley: University of California Press, 1994).
29. Don Gifford, *Joyce Annotated* (Berkeley & Los Angeles: University of California Press, 1982), 110.
30. *The Portable James Joyce*, 201.
31. Kelleher, 'Irish History and Mythology in James Joyce's "The Dead" ', 419.
32. James Joyce, *Ulysses*, The Corrected Text (Harmondsworth: Penguin, 1986), 314.
33. Sir Samuel Ferguson, *Congal*, 186.
34. Alfred Perceval Graves, 'Song of the Ghost', collected in *Fairy and Folk Tales of Ireland*, ed. W. B. Yeats (1888; Dublin: Colin Smythe, 1973), 123.
35. Ibid. 370.
36. James Joyce, *Selected Letters*, ed. Richard Ellmann (New York: Viking, 1957), 18.
37. 'The Dead', 240.
38. Lady Gregory, *Gods and Fighting Men*, 96.
39. 'The Dead', 226.
40. Ibid. 202.
41. Ibid. 214.
42. Ibid. 220–1.
43. Standish O'Grady, *History of Ireland: Critical and Philosophical* (1881).
44. Hyde, 'The Necessity for De-Anglicizing Ireland'.
45. 'The Dead', 207.
46. Jeremiah Curtin, *Myths and Folklore of Ireland* (1890; reissued by Wings Books, 1975), 290.
47. 'The Dead', 201.
48. Ibid. 216–17.
49. Ibid. 220.
50. Ibid. 194.
51. Robert Browning 'Paracelsus', in *The Poems*, i, ed. John Pettigrew (Yale: Yale University Press, 1981).
52. G. K. Chesterton, *Robert Browning* (London: Macmillan, 1903), 182.
53. George Santayana, 'The Poetry of Barbarism', in *Interpretations of Poetry and Religion* (New York: Schribner, 1900), 216.

54. Browning, *Poems*, i. 451.

55. 'The Dead', 237–8.

56. Patrick Kavanagh, *The Complete Poems* (Dublin: Goldsmith, 1972), 238.

57. Ibid. 239.

58. Ibid. 212.

59. W. B. Yeats, Introduction to Lady Gregory, *Gods and Fighting Men*, 17.

60. O'Grady, *History of Ireland: Critical and Philosophical.*

## *Chapter 3*

1. Sheridan Le Fanu, *The House by the Church-Yard* (1861–3; Belfast: Appletree Press, 1992).

2. James Joyce, *Finnegans Wake* (London: Penguin, 1939), 23.

3. Ibid. 528.

4. Richard Ellmann, *James Joyce* (Oxford: Oxford University Press, 1959/1982), 651.

5. Ibid. 650.

6. C. S. Lewis, *The Lion, the Witch and the Wardrobe* (New York: Collier Books 1950/1970), 5–6.

7. Ibid. 7–8.

8. Ibid. 6–7.

9. Ibid. 7.

10. Ibid. 11.

11. Funk and Wagnalls, *Standard Dictionary of Folklore, Mythology and Legend* (New York: Harper Collins 1949/1984), 652.

12. Ibid. 651.

13. *The Lion, The Witch and the Wardrobe*, 10.

14. Funk and Wagnalls, *Standard Dictionary*, 462.

15. Ibid. 602.

16. Art Mac Cumhaigh, *Dánta*, ed. by Tomás Ó Fíaich An Clochomhar (Dublin: published by the editor, 1973), 111.

17. Lady Gregory, *Gods and Fighting Men* (London: John Murray, 1904), 89.

18. *Finnegans Wake*, 179.

19. Mac Cumhaigh, *Danta*, 132.

20. Ibid. 113.

21. *The Portable James Joyce*, ed. Harry Levin (London: Penguin, 1976), 430.

22. *Collected Poems of Thomas MacGreevy*, annotated edn. by Susan Schriebman (Washington: Anna Livia/Catholic University, 1991), 11.

23. Ibid. 12.

24. Ibid. 106.

25. *Letters of Wallace Stevens*, ed. Holly Stevens (New York: Knopf, 1966), 596.

26. *Collected Poems of Thomas MacGreevy*, 19.

27. 'The Dead', *The Portable James Joyce*, 219.

28. Ibid. 232.

29. Ibid. 236.

30. Ibid. 195.

31. Ibid. 200.

32. Ibid. 202.

33. All quotations from P. W. Joyce, 'The Voyage of Mailduin', in *Old Celtic Romances* (London: C. Kegan Paul, 1879), 112–76.

34. Louis MacNeice, *The Mad Islands and The Administrator* (London: Faber, 1964), 7.

35. Ibid. 47.

36. Gerard Murphy, *Early Irish Lyrics* (Oxford: Clarendon Press, 1956), 74.

37. Bevis Hillier, *Young Betjeman* (London: John Murray, 1988), 136.

38. Jon Stallworthy, *Louis MacNeice* (London: Faber, 1995), 31–2.

39. Ibid. 497.

40. P. W. Joyce, *Old Celtic Romances*, 176.

41. Ibid. 165.

42. Louis MacNeice, *The Collected Poems* (London: Faber, 1966), 30.

43. John Keats, *Poetical Works* (Oxford: Oxford University Press, 1956), 213.

44. MacNeice, *The Collected Poems*, 522.

45. Ibid. 503.

46. Ibid.

47. *Collected Poems of Thomas MacGreevy*, 24.

48. MacNeice, *The Collected Poems*, 30.

49. *Collected Poems of Thomas MacGreevy*, 11–13.

50. Quoted by Nicholas Canny, *The Elizabethan Conquest of Ireland* (New York: Barnes and Noble, 1976), 76.

51. 'The Dead', 236.

52. Ibid. 232.

53. Ibid. 233.

54. Ibid. 192.

55. Ibid. 233.

56. Ibid. 240.

57. Ibid. 241.

58. Ibid. 239.

59. Ibid. 238.

60. Ibid. 227.
61. James MacKillop, *Dictionary of Celtic Mythology* (Oxford: Oxford University Press, 1998), 184.
62. Ibid. 253.
63. 'The Dead', 235.
64. Ibid. 233–4.
65. Gerald of Wales, *The History and Topography of Ireland* (London: Penguin, 1982), 110.
66. 'The Dead', 231.
67. Ibid. 233.
68. Ibid. 234.
69. Ibid. 235.
70. Collected in *The Poems and Poetry of Munster* (Dublin: O'Daly, 1849).
71. 'The Dead', 232.
72. Ibid. 235.
73. Ibid. 238.
74. Ibid. 234.
75. *Collected Works of Padraic H. Pearse: Plays, Poems and Stories* (Dublin: Maunsel, 1918).
76. Francis Quarles, *The Complete Works in Prose and Verse* (Edinburgh: Edinburgh University Press, 1880), 145.
77. W. R. Rodgers, *Poems*, ed. and introduced by Michael Longley (Meath, Ireland: Gallery Books, 1993), 98–9.

## Chapter 4

1. Laurence Sterne, *The Life and Opinions of Tristram Shandy, Gentleman*, ed. Graham Petrie (London: Penguin, 1967), 64.
2. Ibid. 68.
3. 'The Dead', in *The Portable James Joyce*, ed. Harry Levin (London: Penguin, 1976), 194.
4. Ibid. 233.
5. Lady Gregory, *Gods and Fighting Men* (London; John Murray, 1904), 293.
6. 'The Dead', 234.
7. Ibid. 193–4.
8. Sir Samuel Ferguson, *Lays of the Western Gael* (London and Dublin, 1897).
9. 'The Dead', 237.
10. Ibid. 240.

11. Ibid. 194.
12. Ibid. 237.
13. Ibid. 241.
14. *Tristram Shandy*, 92.
15. Gilbert Burnet, *History of His Own Time* (London, 1724).
16. *Tristram Shandy*, 293.
17. Jonathan Swift, *The Complete Poems*, ed. Pat Rogers (London: Penguin English Poets, 1983), 221.
18. Ibid. 21.
19. Ibid. 37.
20. Ibid. 563.
21. Ibid. 60.
22. Ibid. 114.
23. Ibid. 451.
24. John Millington Synge, *The Playboy of the Western World* (Dublin: Maunsel, 1907; London: Methuen, 1983).
25. George Petrie, *Ancient Music of Ireland*.
26. Douglas Hyde, *The Love Songs of Connacht* (Dublin: Dun Emer, 1904; Irish University Press, 1971), 3, 7, 9.
27. Ibid. preliminary page.
28. Synge, *The Playboy of the Western World*, 100.
29. George Farquhar, *The Beaux' Stratagem* (Lincoln: University of Nebraska Press, 1977), 44–5.
30. Ibid. 96.
31. John Toland, *A Collection of Several Pieces* (London: 1726), 48.
32. *The Portable Swift*, ed. Carl Van Doren (New York: Penguin, 1976), 254.
33. Ibid. 274.
34. Toland, *Collection*.
35. R. Buick Knox, *James Ussher, Archbishop of Armagh* (Cardiff: University of Wales, 1967).
36. 'The Dead', 227.
37. Charles Vallancey, *An Essay on the Antiquity of the Irish Language* (London, 1822), 71.
38. Ibid. 78–9.
39. Jonathan Swift, *The Drapier's Letters*, ed. Herbert Davis (Oxford: Oxford University Press, 1942), 139.
40. *The Portable Swift*, 411.
41. Ibid. 412.
42. Vallancey, *Essay*, 93–4.

43. W. B. Yeats, Introduction to *Cuchulain of Muirthemne* (New York: Oxford University Press, 1970).

44. *The Collected Letters of W. B. Yeats*, ed. John Kelly, vol. i. (Oxford: Oxford University Press, 1986), 84–8.

45. Ibid. 116.

46. Robert Dwyer Joyce, *Deirdre* (1876; Boston: Roberts Brothers, 1877), 227–8.

47. *Eleven Plays of William Butler Yeats*, ed. A. Norman Jeffares (New York: Collier Books, 1964), 65.

48. 'The Dead', 213.

49. Ibid. 213–14.

50. Ibid. 202.

51. Robert Dwyer Joyce, *Deirdre*, 248.

52. *Eleven Plays of William Butler Yeats*, 72.

53. Ibid. 73.

54. Louis MacNeice, *The Poetry of W. B. Yeats* (New York: Oxford University Press, 1941), 167.

55. Quoted by Richard Ellmann, *The Identity of Yeats* (London: Faber, 1954), 201.

56. *Eleven Plays of W. B. Yeats*, 63–4.

57. *The Collected Poems of W. B. Yeats*, ed. Richard J. Finneran (London: Macmillan, 1989), 307.

58. Quoted in W. B. Yeats, *The Celtic Twilight*, 49.

59. Ibid. 49–50.

60. *The Collected Poems of W. B. Yeats*, 259–60.

61. Swift, *The Complete Poems*, 114.

62. Ibid. 452.

63. Ibid. 455.

# Index